The Architecture of London 2012

VISION > DESIGN > LEGACY

The Architecture of London 2012

VISION > DESIGN > LEGACY

TOM DYCKHOFF & CLAIRE BARRETT

Commissioned photography by Edmund Sumner

An official London 2012 publication

WILEY

For London's glorious East Enders

This edition first published in 2012
Copyright © 2012 John Wiley & Sons

Registered office
John Wiley & Sons Ltd, The Atrium, Southern Gate,
Chichester, West Sussex, PO19 8SQ,
United Kingdom

An official London 2012 publication.

London 2012 emblem(s) © The London Organising Committee of
the Olympic Games and Paralympic Games Ltd (LOCOG) 2007.
All rights reserved.

For details of our global editorial offices, for customer services
and for information about how to apply for permission to reuse
the copyright material in this book please see our website at
www.wiley.com

Front cover image: © ODA; Back cover images: [left] © ODA,
[centre] © Edmund Sumner, [right] © Edmund Sumner.

Wiley publishes in a variety of print and electronic formats and
by print-on-demand. Some material included with standard
print versions of this book may not be included in e-books or in
print-on-demand. If this book refers to media such as a CD or
DVD that is not included in the version you purchased, you may
download this material at http://booksupport.wiley.com. For
more information about Wiley products, visit www.wiley.com.
Designations used by companies to distinguish their products
are often claimed as trademarks. All brand names and product
names used in this book are trade names, service marks,
trademarks or registered trademarks of their respective owners.
The publisher is not associated with any product or vendor
mentioned in this book. This publication is designed to provide
accurate and authoritative information in regard to the subject
matter covered. It is sold on the understanding that the publisher
is not engaged in rendering professional services. If professional
advice or other expert assistance is required, the services of a
competent professional should be sought.

A catalogue record for this book is available
from the British Library.

ISBN 978-1119-99386-5 (paperback);
ISBN 978-1119-97683-7 (ebk); ISBN 978-1119-94150-7; (ebk);
ISBN 978-1119-97685-1 (ebk); 978-1119-97684-4 (ebk)
Typeset in Futura
Designed by www.rawshock.co.uk
Printed in Italy by Printer Trento Srl.

Contents

Foreword		6
Introduction		8
Chapter 1	Plans and Preparations	16
Chapter 2	A Walk in the Park	54
Chapter 3	More than Meets the Eye	148
Chapter 4	Beyond the Valley	186
Chapter 5	Village People	214
Chapter 6	The Show Must Go On	238
Afterword		257
Index		260
Picture Credits		264

Foreword

When Jacques Rogge, the President of the IOC, opened an envelope on 6 July 2005 and said, 'the Games of the 30th Olympiad are awarded to the city of London', the UK was presented with the opportunity to create and deliver something truly distinctive. The window was there to change the approach to the architecture of venues and the temporary infrastructure of events around the world.

The bid presentation delivered by Lord Coe in Singapore that day gave a glimpse of what was to come: a Games that appeals to the youth of the world, with sport at its heart, showcasing London; a sustainable Games where permanent venues would only be built where they could be underpinned by a solid business plan.

In addition to the lasting legacy left by a number of world-class venues, the bid team proposed more temporary venues and infrastructure in London than in any previous Games. This presented the chance to shape a truly unique Games, with major temporary venues in the heart of the capital.

The vision for our venues that we set during the bid was to showcase London's skyline, creating London as the venue for the Olympic and Paralympic Games. We thus selected venue locations with backdrops to London's famous landmarks: Big Ben, Tower Bridge, The London Eye and Buckingham Palace, along with parkland settings such as Greenwich Park, Hyde Park and St James's Park.

London's Olympic Park builds on the rich heritage of London's Royal Parks to deliver a spectacular green space for the twenty-first century and puts in place the building blocks for a sustainable new community. With the rivers and green lawns forming the heart of the Park, London's Olympic Park has been designed not as a large pedestrian concourse, but as a beautiful parkland setting for the venues.

So London 2012 represents a notable shift in approach to the presentation, architecture and design of venues for an Olympic and Paralympic Games. Such an approach is designed to create a memorable Games for spectators, whether for those lucky enough to get tickets or for the potential four billion TV viewers around the world, and venue architecture and settings that will inspire the athletes to achieve their personal best. We have collectively embraced the opportunity to deliver sports venues in settings that may never happen with this level of intensity or scale again, opening views to the city and delivering the magic of the Games in an absolutely unique context.

Building on from the principles of the 2012 bid, the bar was set to challenge preconceived ideas of Games event architecture. A new benchmark could be set in responding to this truly once in a lifetime opportunity. This realisation has driven all teams involved in the design and delivery of the London 2012 Games – bringing together the very best architects, engineers, artists and designers in the world to focus on a single vision. It is through collaboration across all design disciplines that these goals have been achieved, combining the best creative talents available and collective working between all organisations across the piece. Although only a snippet of the overall picture, I hope the insight within whets your appetite to visit, experience and celebrate the architecture of London 2012.

James Bulley
Director of Venues and Infrastructure
London Organising Committee of the Olympic Games and Paralympic Games

It's one thing for a city to win an Olympic and Paralympic Games.

It's quite another actually to make those Games happen. After the euphoria of London's successful bid had died down the real work began and key decisions had to be made. What kind of Games did we want? What would they look like? And, most tricky of all, how would London build quality architecture on time and within budget – and build it to last?

What was more surprising on that heady July day in 2005 when the Host City for the 2012 Olympic and Paralympic Games was announced? That London should have won at all? After all, Paris was favourite. Or that, come 2012, the Games would be held in the Lower Lea Valley in east London? The Lea Valley Games? Who would have thought it? For those who haven't visited, this was not the most obvious spot for an Olympic and Paralympic Games. It had its moments of beauty: walking along the canal on a Sunday afternoon, perhaps, sun

glinting off the surface of the water, blooming buddleia bursting from the verges. But it was not a place used to sporting superstars and the glare of international TV crews. Its neighbourhoods – Hackney Wick, Stratford, Leyton – would never be Beverly Hills or Mayfair. Sure, you would get the odd film crew roaming its streets looking for an edgy location, but this has never been somewhere used to the limelight or, indeed, the attention of billions of people around the world.

Where you now see stadia, plazas and iconic sculptures, another

▲ An aerial view of the Olympic Park in December 2011 looking south. North Greenwich Arena and Canary Wharf are visible in the distance.

landscape existed quite happily for centuries, keeping itself to itself: a landscape of odds and ends. Every city has its Lea Valley, a spot where things that don't fit in elsewhere find their place. It was the archetypical hinterland – London's backroom, where all manner of things went on quietly, far from public gaze.

Never forget, this is a river estuary, where the Lea meets the Thames in rivulets that formed after the last ice age. For thousands of years the muddy, marshy, miasmic Lea Valley was a nuisance for Londoners – a barrier to those escaping the city, whether Roman legions gingerly

▲ A view of the Park site prior to redevelopment. The site had 52 electricity pylons and more than 200 buildings, which were largely industrial sheds.

crossing the 'old ford' (whose name still echoes round these parts) en route for Colchester's garrison or medieval millers heading to market from their watermills. As if in revenge, when, at last, we did manage to tame the marshes, we banished there all the things we'd prefer not to see, or smell: factories, chemical works, sewage pipes, the toxic underbelly of urban civilisation. The Lower Lea Valley, say the archaeologists at the Museum of London, is industrial Britain's 'best kept secret', a 'trailblazer', where the word 'petrol' was coined in 1892, where plastic was invented four decades earlier, where industrial dry cleaning came to Britain. But it was never a place in which many people would choose to linger.

Study a map of London before that day in 2005 and the Lower Lea Valley appears as a gap. The dense scrum of the city to the east, west, north and south suddenly loosens. Racks of Victorian terraced housing give way to great expanses of blank space. Sweeping curls of railway lines fray into sidings, before culminating in rectangles marked 'Depot' or 'Freight Terminal'. Other blocks are marked 'Works'. There were a lot of 'works' in the Lower Lea Valley. There still are, though many died in the 1970s and 1980s with Britain's de-industrialisation and the decline of London's docks, adding to the landscape's history of abandonment – that haunted, post-industrial air so adored by its stalwart supporters, who revel in the Lea Valley's status as urban antihero.

Of course this was no gap in the map. What cartography won't show you are the details only being in a place can reveal. The cheeky plastic sign of Percy Dalton's Peanut Factory. The dog racing track. The vast scrap yards. The kebab meat factory. The infamous 'Hackney fridge mountain' of discarded consumer durables looming over Carpenters Road, now recycled into who knows what. Nor will it reveal the feel of the place, its peculiar combination of the industrial and the pastoral. This was London's last wilderness. You could cycle along towpaths lush with elderflowers and hardly know the city was out there. Nor will it show its history, like the 1888 strike at the Bryant and May match factory – now apartments, but once the birthplace of Britain's labour movement, after women and teenage girls suffering 14-hour days and the pains of 'phossy jaw' said 'no more'.

Nor can cartography show a place's people. This may have been an area of high unemployment and crime, but it was also valued by many. Weekend horticulturalists gathered at the Marsh Lane Allotments; teenagers kicked footballs around and dreamed of playing for West Ham; the car park of the Kingsway Evangelical Church burst into the bloom of a thousand Afro-Caribbean Brits in their Sunday best; a community of travellers laid down roots on the Clays Lane estate; pop singer Michael Hutchence first flirted with Paula Yates live on camera, sprawled on the bed of what was, briefly in the 1990s, the most famous house in Britain, home of the country's most outrageous TV show, 'The Big Breakfast'. They may both have passed away, but the house is still there, a home once again, though hidden from the cameras these days at the end of Dace Road.

And yet it is here, of all places, right here, on this shy, in-between, dirty old spot that London 2012 has chosen to hold the greatest show on earth.

▼ The 'Hackney Fridge Mountain' was a 6m-high pile of discarded white goods that was recycled to create a pop-up cinema called Films on Fridges.

7

plans and preparations

An Olympic and Paralympic Games has to go somewhere.

Once a city decides to put itself forward to host a Games, it has to get down to the nitty gritty of where to put it. Talk to a town planner these days, and the experience from decades of planning mistakes tells us that a city evolves slowly, that if you're going to add anything big to the city, don't do as we did in the 1960s and sledgehammer it in. Nowadays the buzz words in urbanism are 'stitch', 'weave' and 'knit', what early twentieth-century city planner Patrick Geddes called 'conservative surgery'.

The Lower Lea Valley

But you can't knit, stitch or weave an Olympic and Paralympic Games. It is too big, too fast. A giant chunk of London had to be turned from shrinking violet to A-list star poised for the international cameras in five years. The Games are a hulking great beast. They are accompanied by legions of stuff – organisations, expectations, international politics, security worries. They come with a bullish, in-built momentum. Planned poorly, an Olympic and Paralympic Games can ruin a city, bankrupting it, knocking it about with bulldozers, relocating lives for buildings that might look good on the cameras but that nobody wants a week after the TV crews have gone home.

So where in this dense, layered city of lives were we going to put the Games? Head west? That made sense, given that Heathrow Airport and Lord Foster's freshly rebuilt Wembley Stadium sit on that side of the city. 'It was a natural starting point,' says Alison Nimmo, Director of Design and Regeneration at the Olympic Delivery Authority (ODA), the public body responsible for developing and building the new venues and infrastructure for the Games and their use after 2012. Plus there were the historical links to the London 1908 Games, held nearby in

▲ London hosted its first Olympic Games in 1908. Located in White City, the event took place within existing buildings, including the Franco-British Exhibition Stadium designed the same year.

White City. 'But there just wasn't enough space,' she adds. An Olympic and Paralympic Games needs a huge area, yet one not so far out on a limb that people couldn't get to it. Now, where in London would we find a place like that?

The Lower Lea Valley tempted for more than just reasons of space. It was cut off, with rivers and canals east and west, the busy, brutish A12 to the north and a mainline railway to the south – good for security, even if this isolation had contributed to its recent decline. That in turn, though, presented an opportunity. This was a part of London that had so far stubbornly refused to regenerate in the economic boom of the early 2000s. The four boroughs surrounding it – Hackney, Newham, Tower Hamlets and Waltham Forest – are still among the two per cent of the poorest in the country. And there was little prospect of any change, remembers Nimmo. There were dozens of regeneration plans flying around for the area, but 'none of them had seen the light of day,' she says. The Lower Lea Valley was blighted with land seriously contaminated from centuries of the foulest industries and a constellation of small, short-let landowners. In short, a big bill, with nobody willing or able to pick up the tab. The site did have potential, though: great transport links, proximity to central London. 'There was a big strategic opportunity there,' says Nimmo. 'But you needed something to kickstart it, to attract serious money and confidence into a part of London that

The first physical evidence that the Games had arrived in London was the bright blue fence that ran around the perimeter of the site.

had suffered for years from a lack of investment and decline.'

Step forward London's Mayor at the time of the bid, Ken Livingstone. Livingstone was a 'love him or hate him' figure, as mayors generally are. His singular cocktail of politics, 'socialist capitalism', perhaps – courting property developers one minute, taxing 4x4s the next – did divide opinion. But by 2003, when he became involved in London's bid, it was starting to work. The city had an economic and cultural confidence it hadn't had in decades. 'And Ken was adamant,' remembers Nimmo: 'the Games had to be in east London.'

Olympic and Paralympic Games make things happen. Buildings that might take twice the time to construct are whipped up in lightning speed. Things get done. 'When you do an urban planning masterplan,' says Jerome Frost, Head of Design at the ODA, 'it's normally delivered in 25 years. We've done it in five.' The trick is to harness that bullish momentum so that it ends up benefiting the city, rather than leaving a damaging trail in its wake.

Decision number two: what *kind* of Games to have. One that simply passes through, with few permanent physical legacies, like Atlanta 1996? Or one that leaves hundreds of reminders, utterly transforming the fortunes of a city, like Barcelona 1992? A Games that trumpets its green credentials, like Sydney 2000? Something iconic and monumental, like Beijing 2008? A little bit of all four, as it happens.

London 2012 definitely knew what kind of Games *not* to have, one that almost bankrupted a city by building too ambitiously, like Montreal 1976, and, especially, one that left behind those tricky beasts – white elephants. Both Athens and Beijing have suffered by building venues that had no real purpose after the Games ended in 2004 and 2008 respectively.

Of course, most of the public attention focused at first on the sleek look of the bid's masterplan; its 'iconic' buildings worked like catnip on the British press. Zaha Hadid's Aquatics Centre was part of this original bid. Awarded through an international design competition, the project came with a commitment from Mayor Livingstone, recalls Frost, 'to the IOC [International Olympic Committee] that we're going to do something whether we win or not.' 'Zaha's building was a statement of confidence, quality and ambition,' adds Nimmo. 'These iconic structures are the ones that capture the public's imagination.' 'Zaha magic', she calls it.

▶ RIGHT: Santiago Calatrava's communication tower at Barcelona's 1992 Olympic Games became a symbol for the event, as well as a lasting reminder of the city's regeneration brought about by the Games.

▶ FAR RIGHT: The incredible tensile-roof structure engineered by Frei Otto for the 1972 Munich Olympic Games dramatically swoops and lifts to cover all the main sporting venues.

▶ BOTTOM RIGHT: Sold on architectural razzmatazz, Athens commissioned architect Santiago Calatrava to design its Olympic Sports Complex for the 2004 Olympic and Paralympic Games.

But London didn't win the bid because of its looks. It succeeded, first, stated the IOC, because of what London and Britain could offer the Olympic and Paralympic Games. Lord Coe, Chair of the London 2012 bid company, gave a passionate speech that pledged to put youth at the heart of the Games, and to guarantee their success thanks to this country's obsession with sport. 'We could give the Games back in better shape,' explains Nimmo. 'It's why London pipped Paris to the finish line at the eleventh hour.'

Second, London won because of its plans for 'legacy': its far-reaching ambitions to use the Games to transform a city. The last two times London had hosted the Olympic Games it was more by default than by design. In 1908 it replaced Rome at the last minute, when Mount Vesuvius erupted; in 1948 Britain stood forward, despite being mired in austerity, to gee up a world recovering from the Second World War. There was a make do and mend approach to both events. This time round, though, we'd host the Games with gusto.

For the ODA, the real inspiration, in terms of architecture and design, was Barcelona 1992, in how it both integrated the show *and* the Games experience into the city fabric. The Games were used as a catalyst for change, fast-tracking a 30-year blueprint to put the entire city on a new path, through massive investment in infrastructure. Work that would otherwise have taken decades was rattled off in a mere five years. Before the Games, Barcelona was in typical post-industrial decline, worsened by decades of under-investment under General Franco as revenge for its opposition during the Spanish Civil War. It was a city, though, with a proud history – only just manifest in its dark, shabby streets.

Two decades on, Barcelona has become the poster boy for urban regeneration around the world. Thronging with international tourists, its Olympic sporting venues are still very much in use. The city has managed successfully to harness that Games momentum for decades afterwards. How have they done it? By seeing the Games as a motor behind a coherent long-term plan for the city. How an Olympic and Paralympic Games integrates itself into its Host City is absolutely crucial to whether or not the Games just come and go without leaving a mark, or, worse, leave a damaging scar – or whether they transform the landscape for good.

PLANNING TO WIN

So what kind of physical legacy does London 2012 promise to leave behind? A huge new Olympic Park amid the River Lea's tributaries, world-class sports venues, impressive architecture: that's all to be expected. But what of its underlying philosophy? London 2012 decided upon several core values right from the start. For instance,

accessibility would be built into the design of the Park as a completely normal, unnoticeable thing, not an added extra. This was a legal requirement following the Disability Discrimination Act. It was also crucial to the values of the Olympic and Paralympic Movements and felt especially appropriate given that the roots of the Paralympic Games were formed after the Second World War in Britain, at Stoke Mandeville Hospital. Indeed, those legal requirements were often not enough. Sports wheelchairs, for instance, are far larger than conventional wheelchairs, needing greater space. Though, says Kevin Owens, Design Principal at the London Organising Committee of the Olympic Games and Paralympic Games (LOCOG), the body responsible for preparing and staging the 2012 Games, designing the entire Park from the outset with the Paralympic Games – which follow the Olympic Games – as an equal was novel. To the Park's designers, the Paralympic Games are simply another Games 'mode', with its own demands and demographic (generally more child- and family-focused) to which the venues have to adapt.

Indeed, it's that kind of adaptability that is *the* core philosophy behind the whole of London 2012's architecture. From the outset, the intention was to build both for the Games and for its legacy in the years afterwards. A city evolves and adapts, so whatever you add to it has to evolve and adapt, too. Key for Jerome Frost, the ODA's

◀ An overview of the entire site once work had begun to clear the land, with the A12 skirting round its northern perimeter.

Head of Design, is that such 'flexibility' was built into the Park from the very start: 'It means we tried not to preclude or prevent something happening in the future. We've created a place that can change quite dramatically after the Games.' The Park you see now is designed to be radically changed once London 2012 has moved on (p.238).

Such complex flexibility requires meticulous scheduling. The site has to be planned for the short term – the Games themselves – but also the long term – the months, years and decades post-Games. Ultimately the plan's success depends upon how well these timescales are knitted together. You start, says Alison Nimmo, with the long term: 'working out where we want to get to in legacy, and how do you get there.' You decide what this part of the city will need in years to come. For instance, why be stuck with an inflexible arena designed for thousands to watch Hockey during the Games, when you know in five years time it will be disused? Before you build anything, question whether you need to build at all. Maybe there are other buildings or venues you could adapt. A huge number of events are taking place not in the Park, but in existing prominent sporting venues, such as Hampden Park, Glasgow, or in historic sites such as Greenwich Park, Wimbledon, Wembley or Hadleigh Farm, Essex (p.186), to embed the Games in the whole nation and take advantage of each place's heritage. If you must build anew, decide whether you're building for the short term or the long term. Many of the venues – such as the Riverbank Arena and the Basketball Arena – are only there for the Games. Afterwards they will be dismantled, their parts recycled or reused and the land underneath developed as new quarters of the city. These are designed to stitch and weave and knit the city around it into the Olympic Park, and vice versa, rather than leaving the Park and its features isolated.

Finally, whatever is built to last, build it well; and build it, too, to change swiftly after the Games have ended. Take the Olympic and Paralympic Village. When the Games end, its blocks will be turned into everyday housing. The mentality behind the Village was to plan it from the outset to be an instant, ordinary part of the city – with a school, shops and a health centre – which just happened to be adapted for an Olympic and Paralympic Games for a few weeks in 2012.

Next, you begin with the behind-the-scenes stuff: you build the infrastructure and you make good land contaminated from many years of industrial use. The ODA had to create 'oven-ready sites', as Nimmo calls them, that could be easily adapted in the future, with pipes and service ducts, say, with room for more cabling as it is needed, or a site-wide green energy system to plug into. You make sure the Park connects with surrounding investment, such as Crossrail, London's up-and-coming cross-city rail line, and developer Westfield's vast shopping centre at Stratford City, which – though a missed opportunity architecturally

▲ The Basketball Arena is one of the temporary venues on the Olympic Park, aimed at avoiding any 'white elephants' when the Games is over.

– delivers shops, hotels, entertainment and leisure facilities to a site beside the Park. Such forward thinking and investment in infrastructure is extremely rare in the UK, a country normally plagued with short-term thinking. Only the Games' public funding, and a national government to underwrite it, made such an audacious leap possible.

Such planning for change adds a crucial extra few layers of complexity to a blueprint already mind-numbingly complex. Not only must you demolish what's there already, prepare the site, lay down the infrastructure, plan the Games, build the venues and hold the event; but also you have to plot the future outline of a whole chunk of a city that doesn't even exist yet. You have to be an urban clairvoyant.

The Olympic Park Legacy Company (OPLC) was founded in 2009 to create the blueprint for the Queen Elizabeth Olympic Park, as it will be renamed after London 2012, which will reopen in phases from 2013 (p.238). This, in itself, is quite an achievement. Sydney did not get a body focused on legacy until two years after the Games. The only previous Games where the future has been integrated so early on is Barcelona 1992.

Yet even before the OPLC came into being, the ODA had to design a Park filled with venues, says Jerome Frost, that felt like a readymade 'piece of the city', poised to slot into London, a tough job in a city of constant change. 'For example, with the Copper Box [an arena hosting

Handball, the fencing element of the Modern Pentathlon and Goalball during the Games that becomes a neighbourhood leisure centre afterwards], it's neat, compact, unassuming. It thinks about its setting. We don't want it detracting from what Hackney Wick already has to offer – its artists, small businesses, lots of different nationalities. We don't want it to stand out and set everything else apart,' he says. It's vital for the Park to embrace the surrounding neighbourhoods, reckons Sir Nicholas Serota, Director of the Tate (responsible for architects Herzog & de Meuron's lauded conversion of Bankside Power Station into Tate Modern) and a key ODA Board member: 'The junction between old and new is critical. The ODA has tried to do certain things that will ensure that junction works as well as it can – the legacy company will have to ensure that.'

It's a difficult job. Little survives of the old Lea Valley inside the Park, aside from the River Lea itself, and a few Victorian fragments: the canal, the odd railway bridge and one small building – an early twentieth-century warehouse that has been retained and will form part of the new Energy Centre in the west. 'One of the issues,' explains Serota, 'is that there was so little within the former site that was worth keeping.' While outside the Park, a small Olympic and Paralympic outreach programme has invested in local sports facilities that will be used as training venues for the athletes during the Games. Such initiatives have helped to avoid a stark divide between the developments in the Park and its surrounding area. Nonetheless, given how much had to be achieved so quickly, and how vast a behemoth the Games is, it is perhaps inevitable that the landscape inside the Park has been the primary concern.

A SUSTAINABLE GAMES

Soon after London won the bid, reality kicked in. The bid's seductive design 'was really important for the glitzy, glamorous area of marketing,' admits Selina Mason, Deputy Head of Design at the ODA, with some candour. 'Then you win it and there's that moment when you're faced with the enormity of the task ahead!' she laughs. Dreams are all well and good, but how are we going to build them, and, crucially, who's going to pay?

What a good job, then, that flexibility and change were key driving principles for London 2012's design from the start, because from July 2005 onwards it has had to cope with nothing but change, both inside and, more crucially, outside: a new London Mayor, Boris Johnson, from the Conservative Party in 2008; a new National Coalition government in 2010; and, most seriously of all, the world financial crisis that broke in 2007. Even before the economic crisis, though, the Games' cost became a key political issue – as it always

▲ An external view of the Olympic Stadium in October 2011. Its design sums up the London 2012 design philosophy: adaptability, affordability, sustainability and deliverability.

does, whoever is the Host City – increasingly so as concerns grew about exactly what public money was to be spent on.

What we now needed, says Sir Nicholas Serota, was 'a sustainable and affordable Games, an ambition to do something clearly different than what was developing in Beijing, at a level of cost that could be afforded not only by the UK but by other countries going forward.' This had to be a Games that mainly paid for itself.

The shadow of Wembley Stadium's rebuilding also loomed large. At the time of the bid, the new stadium was a political embarrassment, going wildly over budget and schedule. Years on, we are so used to the Games' building programme being not just on time but often ahead of schedule it is easy to forget the very public drubbing over key national building projects, such as Wembley, the Scottish Parliament and the Millennium Dome, that went before it. 'The first three years were very challenging,' remembers Nimmo. 'No-one thought we could do it. People were saying it was going to be a national disgrace, that our stadium would be flatpack and so and so.' The London 2012 Games would be the mega-project that Britain actually built without fiasco, that drew a new line in the sand.

Alongside adaptability and design quality, two further concepts now became part of the ODA's philosophy: affordability and deliverability – how to beat down costs and make sure what was planned could

▶ With just two years to go until the Games, a celebration is held on the Olympic Park where the major buildings are well underway. However, the only evidence of the Aquatics Centre is its incredible roof.

actually be built, and on time. They set the tone for appointing the architects, designers and contractors, and for only building permanent venues that had a long-term use.

Zaha Hadid's Aquatics Centre is the only building inherited by the ODA from the 2005 bid, Hadid having been signed up through an international design competition early on. It had to be rethought to suit these new ODA philosophies. So as not to be left with a permanent swimming venue with the 17,500 capacity needed for the Games – beautiful, but too big to be practical in the long term; swimming rarely attracts such crowds – it had to be redesigned, a compromise found. Most of the money has been spent on the lavishly designed, iconic permanent building seating 2,500, into which two temporary seating stands have been slotted for the Games themselves – a practical solution, though it's only in legacy that the building will look at its best.

However, from now on the ODA decided it wanted for the Olympic Park architecture of a different kind to that offered by Hadid: not so much stand-out statement buildings, but, says Nimmo, 'moments of excellence, in a subtle way'. Hadid's building was also the only one to be put out to international competition. 'After that we were looking for teams,' she says, so that the relationship between the architect who designed the project and the contractor who built it – crucial to make

sure it was delivered on time and on budget – was sealed from the start.

After the pomp of Beijing 2008, there was a conscious move against the iconic building, it having arguably reached its apotheosis. 'Once we'd worked out how to follow Beijing, it was straightforward. Beijing was about a nation coming of age. It was about China – a statement of national identity. Being a bit more modest about *our* goals gave us confidence.'

If Beijing 2008 was to be all about excess, a last blow-out before the stock market slump of September 2008, London 2012 would be about building responsibly. Sustainability was a philosophy fixed upon from the start. Experts BioRegional wrote sustainability into the bid document. Its director, Sue Riddlestone, notes that London's mayor at the time, Ken Livingstone, prioritised the issue. Such top-level commitment was vital. There have been many compromises along the way, as plans

▲ The apotheosis of the iconic building, the 'Bird's Nest' Olympic Stadium was constructed for the 2008 Beijing Games.

became reality. The high-profile 120m wind turbine, for example, was cancelled for reasons of health and safety. Yet, says Riddlestone, the key achievement of the Games is not in such grandiose statements and 'eco-bling', but in 'embedding' and 'mainstreaming' sustainability in everything London 2012 does, 'making it a completely normal thing in the construction industry, an astonishing thing in such a vast, complex beast'. The Games' *Towards a One Planet 2012* mission statement got the backing of WWF – a coup – with its holistic message based around five aims: encouraging healthy living; social inclusion (creating local jobs and training opportunities); stimulating local biodiversity; minimising waste; and minimising greenhouse gas emissions. From the start, these principles were written into every aspect of even the smallest of contracts. As a result London 2012's success in sustainability is more in what you don't see than what you do. Instead of wind turbines, for instance, a proportion of the Park's energy comes from biomass boilers in the new Energy Centre. A massive 98 per cent of the materials from the buildings demolished on the Olympic Park have been reused or recycled.

The launch of the Olympic Stadium's design allowed the ODA to announce its own distinct design philosophy, so different from that of Beijing 2008. The Stadium, in one building, encapsulated the new approach – adaptability, affordability (it is designed so it can be reduced post-Games, when it no longer needs to house such vast

▲ A mammoth project like an Olympic and Paralympic Games does not come without its problems. The key to its success has been engagement with the local community from the outset.

◀ The Clays Lane Estate in Stratford, east London, was demolished to make way for the Games.

numbers), sustainability (built with a mere quarter of the steel used in Beijing's stadium) and deliverability, but also design elegance, all wrapped up in one very British word, thinks Selina Mason – economy. 'Our architectural vision is very British,' she says, 'about an economy of means. Not economy for its own sake, but there is an aesthetic that goes along with it that's an English [sic] aesthetic. There is a strong sense of integrity about what architecture means beyond itself, how architecture impacts both environmentally and socially.'

THE DESIGN CHAMPION
Sir Nicholas Serota

Sir Nicholas Serota's credentials for major building projects are impressive. He's famous for employing Swiss superstars Herzog & de Meuron to transform Bankside power station into Tate Modern in 2000, a commission that no doubt helped the architects hit the big time, winning architecture's biggest award – the Pritzker Prize – the following year and going on to design Beijing's iconic Olympic Stadium in 2008. Team that with his former role as a chair of the Commission for Architecture and the Built Environment's (CABE) Design Review panel, and an 'increasing interest in the public realm' and Serota was deemed the man for the job, joining the ODA Board in 2006 to help with the selection of architects and developing the masterplan. He was appointed Design Champion for both LOCOG and the ODA in a bid to strength the integration of the two organisations. His mission? 'The Games are a moment when we are showing leadership to the world,' he says, 'a world which is shaped by architects. We should employ the best possible to show the difference that can be made by good architecture and design.' Despite steering through some choppy waters, overall, Serota seems happy with the architecture – 'I think there are several good buildings,' he says. Yet he believes it's the Park as a whole that should be regarded as the real achievement. What he takes away from the project is a 'belief that the public realm is as important as buildings, in fact more important.'

DESIGN MATTERS

London 2012's philosophy was clear: flexibility, economy, affordability, accessibility, deliverability and sustainability. The real challenge, though, was not just to make the Park happen, but to make it of good quality, to capture the romance of those alluring images that helped win the bid. That's one almighty balancing act.

Aside from Hadid and Hopkins Architects (designers of the Velodrome), the architects selected for most of London 2012 are not famous names, but solid practices with good track records in delivering big projects on time and budget, such as Make, Wilkinson Eyre and Populous. 'It would have been challenging to go with an outfit that has only been together for three years to deliver, say, the third largest building on site,' says Kevin Owens, Design Principal at LOCOG. 'More than 50 per cent of the decision making was weighted in design, but a lot of it was about risk and deliverability.' Yet Jerome Frost believes 'we ended up with probably the best of the British architecture crop in my opinion. Generally we've received praise.'

In this climate, there has clearly been a fight to ensure design stays as close to the top of the agenda as possible. 'In the context of huge pressure on time and budgets,' says Selina Mason, 'we needed strong champions promoting quality and good design, but without extravagance.' She had on her side the support of high-profile figures in the building industry, such as Lord Rogers and Ricky Burdett, Professor of Urban Studies at the London School of Economics. But it is perhaps Tate director Sir Nicholas Serota who has played the largest role. 'He has been our guru, champion and inspiration through thick and thin!' Nimmo confesses. 'He's not an architect, but has huge experience in commissioning architecture,' says Owens. 'He was the right person in cultural terms. The Games is not just a sporting event, but a real piece of London with a cultural legacy. With selection quite heavily weighted towards engineering and the technical, Nick brought balance.'

Serota's role has been that of key design champion, 'to support the team in daily battles on design questions,' he explains. 'They're in meetings with people that only care about cost and delivery. To keep arguing that design matters in those circumstances is very hard. Yet the Games enable us to point the way forward to a global audience. We should employ the best possible architects to show the difference that can be made by good architecture.' Good design doesn't necessarily cost more, he says. 'It's about delivering a result that serves its purpose better than any other. I don't think bog standard would have been cheaper than the buildings we have. In many cases designers have used brilliance to save huge sums of money.'

Serota, though, would have liked the selection process to be braver.

▲ The Skylon, designed by rising stars Powell and Moya, was a centrepiece and symbol of the Festival of Britain in 1951. Anish Kapoor's Orbit was commissioned to perform the same function – time will tell if it succeeds.

▶ Given the scale and ambition of London 2012, comparisons have been made with the Festival of Britain held on London's South Bank in 1951, which commissioned some of the country's most talented young architects and designers.

'That's not to say they're not good buildings, but we could have been bolder. I don't feel apologetic about the buildings we've commissioned. But we've not seen the political lead like Herbert Morrison at the Festival of Britain, which ensured design went all the way down to the furnishings.'

'We often use the Festival of Britain as a reference point,' counters LOCOG's Kevin Owens, 'but the biggest difference is that the Festival of Britain was the celebration of a nation, not an Olympic Games event. This is a commercial event. We're in a fundamentally different era. Everything is a commercial proposition.' Exactly. The world financial crisis, when it broke in 2007–2008, only added to the emphasis on deliverability and affordability. Costs had to be cut further, especially when the Olympic and Paralympic Village – originally to be funded privately – suddenly needed public investment. Such financial accountability – to live within our means – takes on a new sensitivity in a recession.

However, roles *have* been found in the Park for smaller or more leftfield designers, architects and artists. Young Scottish firm NORD has created one of the most memorable buildings with its Electricity Substation. Artists such as Tomas Klassnik and Martin Richman have had their work woven into the Park's very fabric as part of the ODA's Art in the Park programme. The Klassnik Corporation, We Made That and Riitta Ikonen are up and coming designers and artists who collaborated to develop Fantasticology on The Greenway. Part of an innovative commission to integrate art into the Park, it has given a valuable stage to a variety of creative individuals and organisations. This is a welcome opportunity, as it is nigh on impossible today for smaller or more ambitious firms to win a big commission solo when deliverability and track record are vital criteria for selection. To be considered, they must have turnover and professional indemnity insurance that stacks up against the scale of the project. Put frankly, they carry with them a risk that they will not deliver on time and on budget.

This situation led to several consortia where bigger practices teamed up with smaller ones that were seen to add creative spark – headline-grabbing Heatherwick Studio, famous for designing London's new Routemaster bus, as well as the UK Pavilion at the Shanghai Expo 2010, for example, collaborated with sports experts FaulknerBrowns Architects on a design for the VeloPark. Unsuccessful in that instance, Thomas Heatherwick will be undoubtedly pleased with his appointment to design the Olympic Cauldron, which will host the Flame throughout the Games. The commission isn't small fry – the Opening Ceremony will be watched by millions.

Yet, in this particular case, the best building won. Perhaps of all the venues of the Park, it is Hopkins Architects' Velodrome that truly shines. One of the first of the venues to be completed, and high on its hill overlooking the busy A12 route out of London, it had already captured the public's enthusiasm (and a nickname, The Pringle) and garnered design awards more than a year before the Games were due to start. This one building embodies like no other the London 2012 watchwords: pragmatism, affordability, deliverability, sustainability and design elegance. And it encapsulates that architectural quality so central to the Games and to architecture as a discipline: economy.

Architecture cannot lie: it is always an expression of the circumstances, good or bad, into which it is born. Over the past seven years, London 2012 has had to cope with radically shifting agendas – political *and* economic. It has been a steep learning curve for all involved. Its architecture reflects that. The eagle-eyed can see the shift written into the Park's very fabric. Those venues begun early on, under different circumstances, such as the Aquatics Centre, or those designed before their future purpose in legacy had been finalised, like the Olympic Stadium (p.58), have had to be radically adapted along the way, with some compromise; excusable, given the enormous pressure to crack on with building. But the very best buildings in the Olympic Park, such as the Velodrome, shine because they have had the clearest, most sensible brief about what they are, and what they will be in years to come, worked out from the word go.

AND FINALLY – THE GAMES

For those four weeks in 2012, though, few people will be thinking about legacy or how the venues got built. They will be thinking, quite rightly, about the Olympic and Paralympic Games. What will the Opening Ceremony be like? Who will win the 400m? How am I going to get to the Games? Are they going to be fun?

There is a final layer to be added to the story of the Olympic Park – the very reason for it existing, the Olympic and Paralympic Games themselves. The Organising Committee of the London 2012 Olympic and Paralympic Games, LOCOG, was set up to run the Games. The ODA was then established to design and construct elements which were handed over when complete. This separation between the ODA, which delivers the majority of the venues and infrastructure, and LOCOG, which runs the Games, is not unique to London 2012, says LOCOG's Design Principal, Kevin Owens. But their integration and their collaboration is.

▲ The Velodrome is one of the Park's great successes. It was designed to the London 2012 brief and prepared from the outset for legacy use.

Creating the overlay for the Games demands more than a merely superficial layer. One bad design decision at this stage and all the ODA's hard work in laying the foundations for the future could be damaged irrevocably. You can design all the brilliant venues you want, but visitors and sportspeople won't forget getting lost in the Park because the signing is all wrong, or queuing for hours for the loos, or what a mess the Park looked because of all those poorly designed banners – possible disasters to avoid at all costs.

Owens, who trained as an architect, is the man in charge, responsible for everything from compiling design briefs for the sporting venues in tandem with the ODA to the design of these temporary elements, from places to grab a bite to eat, sponsors' pavilions and medal podiums right down to the London 2012 pens sold in the shops. Much of his

▲ The steel frame for the Olympic Stadium under construction in 2008. In just six years, the site has been transformed into a huge new Park that contains some of the UK's finest sporting venues.

early work for the Games, though, was spent being pragmatic. His was the clear head that 'remodelled plans into what is deliverable,' he says, 'and put together a clear strategy for the way we were going to design the venues.' Next they had to approach it from the spectators' point of view, thinking 'about where people sit, the quality of the facilities they will use, and the catering.' Finally, all these temporary elements had to be united under one design umbrella, the London 2012 brand, so that wherever you are during the Games – in Weymouth and Portland for the Sailing, in Glasgow for the Football or anywhere in the Park itself – there was one common 'feel' and standard of quality. It is all about that nebulous quality, the experience, from reading this book, or sitting in the Water Polo Arena, to buying Wenlock and Mandeville, the London 2012 mascots, for the kids.

Again, the team needed to be one with enough experience to deliver 34 competition venues. From more than 40 architecture practices, three were selected to form Team Populous: Populous, designers of the Olympic Stadium, which has enormous experience creating sports venues, alongside two big British firms with good track records on that all important on-time, on-budget delivery, Allies and Morrison and Lifschutz Davidson Sandilands.

'Best of British' is the theme of the overlay. This extends from the decision to use historic landscapes – such as Horse Guards Parade and

▲ The waterways have historically been a key part of the area, but in recent years they have been neglected. For London 2012, though, the local river network was used to transport many of the building materials and waste products.

Wembley Stadium, recognisable around the world and tapping into British Heritage – to creating a design vocabulary ('imagine a mix', he says, 'of a music festival, Wimbledon and Chelsea Flower Show'), right down to employing young British design talent to design, says Owens, 'the little "expo" pieces that people will remember', alongside lighting, wayfinding and signage structures and the like – some of which will have real presence at 10–15m tall. Students from London's Royal College of Art, for instance, have designed the medal podia, a brilliant opportunity to broadcast around the world the work of this innovative design incubator. Promising young architecture practice Glowacka Rennie has designed the Truce Wall, on which every athlete signs their pledge to help find peaceful and diplomatic solutions to today's global conflicts, though, alas, this is in a part of the Park, the Olympic and Paralympic Village, accessible only to the athletes and officials, and to their friends and family. A large part of the landscaping to the south of the Park alongside the Greenway provided a big break for the creative collaboration of the Klassnik Corporation, We Made That and Riitta Ikonon. Known as Fantasticology, the wildflower meadow has brought a range of big name, local and up-and-coming artists and designers to the fore. It has also added depth to the Park through 'moments of curiosity', as designer Tomas Klassnik calls them.

The biggest challenge of all for Owens has been to quality control the design of the temporary units of thousands of external companies – from caterers to sellers of merchandise to sponsors – setting up camp in the Park and getting them to embrace London 2012's design values, and to use this opportunity to employ younger, more leftfield British talent. Much of this has been down to negotiating one-on-one with the companies. Owens has also been able to create a design blueprint to which companies must adhere, such as forming four zones, each with a distinct design vocabulary and feel, and outlawing big monolithic temporary structures in favour of ones with a 10m frontage, so as to foster the festival atmosphere.

At the time of writing (late 2011), most details of this vital overlay have not been finalised. It will be up to you, the reader, to look around and see if it has been successful – and if, indeed, the design of the whole London 2012 Olympic and Paralympic Games has been successful. The distinguishing mark of good architecture, after all, is whether it embraces its user with gusto. But, while exploring the Park and making up your mind, do think about all that has been achieved. Compromises have been made, for sure. But think, too, about the scale and the quality of what has been built so quickly, so efficiently and – in the big scheme of things – quite astonishingly without gaffe. And be proud. It's not, these days, an emotion Britain is used to or comfortable with. But on this special occasion, perhaps we can permit it.

▶ NEXT PAGE: An aerial view of the Olympic Park and Stratford on 19 November 2011.

The Olympic Park, straddling the River Lea, is the main stage for the Games.

Here the bulk of the sporting action takes place. It is where you'll find most of the architectural action, too, in venues both permanent and temporary. Parks, though, are as much about their landscape and setting as what they contain, especially this one. Long after the Games have ended, London will be left not only with a new chunk of the city, dotted with quality sports venues, but also with an even greater legacy, a beautiful park of gardens and innovative art. Let us show you round…

Park Icons

The high profile Olympic Stadium, Velodrome and Aquatics Centre give life to the entire Olympic Park. At the south-eastern entrance, where more than two-thirds of visitors arrive, the Aquatics Centre forms a dramatic gateway. At the northern end, the Velodrome perches proudly on its hill. Given Team GB's success in Swimming and Track Cycling at recent Games, it is not surprising that these two disciplines will be well housed, in buildings with intriguingly different architectural approaches. In between, right at the heart of the Park, is the Olympic Stadium – the stunning backdrop to the Opening and Closing Ceremonies that takes to the limelight in a completely new way. Capturing the imagination with their dramatic architecture, these buildings are compelling, unmissable structures, designed by architects at the peak of their game.

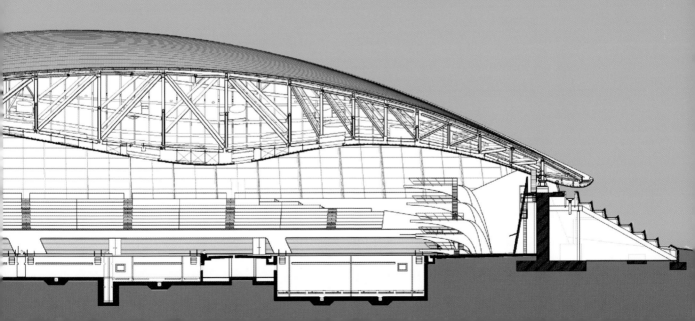

Olympic Stadium

It may look vast and immovable, but the Olympic Stadium was designed to shrink from the beginning. It is a 'semi-temporary building', says its architect, Rod Sheard, Senior Principal at Populous, a firm with one of the longest track records in designing sports venues. Such a plan for a stadium, especially an Olympic and Paralympic one, is unusual. It challenges the very idea of a permanent monument, impressive during the Games and functioning in magnificent style for decades afterwards. Yet, like the Aquatics Centre beside it, the Stadium has been designed to reduce in capacity after the Games. Why? To start with, London does not need a permanent stadium for 80,000 – it has Wembley already which, had it not been on the other side of the city, might have played an even bigger role in the London 2012 Games. So, to avoid being burdened with a white elephant, the thinking when the Stadium was originally commissioned was that a smaller stadium of 25,000 – for athletics, proposed LOCOG's chair, Lord Coe – was far more practical in the long term. Yet during the Olympic and Paralympic Games it still needs to house, excite and inspire a capacity crowd of 80,000. How do you build both?

GAMES CAPACITY
80,000

SPORTS/EVENTS
Athletics, Paralympic Athletics, Opening Ceremonies, Closing Ceremonies

DESIGN INNOVATION
Using just 10,000 tonnes of steel, this is the lightest Olympic Stadium ever built.

EXTRAORDINARY FACT
Much of the steel used for the roof truss is surplus stock wastage from the steel industry; the landscaping features old granite blocks reclaimed from London's King George V Dock when London City Airport was expanded.

PLANNED FUTURE USE
Mixed-use sport with athletics at its core, and wider community use and entertainment. Its capacity will be scaled back to approximately 60,000.

▶ The Olympic Stadium is the first of its scale in the world designed to be 'semi-temporary'. Most of what you see was planned to be disassembled after the Games.

The experience of Rod Sheard and Populous on previous sports venues, such as New York's Yankee Stadium and Stadium Australia for the Sydney 2000 Games, was a great asset. 'We understood what we were getting ourselves into,' Sheard explains, 'we understood the building type very well, which freed us to think in a lateral way.' As well as Sydney's 'conventional' Olympic Stadium, Populous had already designed buildings that could be adapted after use, their capacity decreased. 'So many events around the world could benefit from a "lighter" approach. We have explored temporary buildings made out of shipping containers and scaffolding, recycled timber and plastics.' But designing a stadium that could shrink by around two-thirds was a challenge on a different scale.

Populous brought in as engineer Buro Happold, and as consultant an architect who knows all about adaptable buildings. Peter Cook was one of the founders of Archigram in the 1960s, a young band of architects who dreamt of buildings that used the highest of technology, whose shapes mutated according to the needs and desires of their users. They came up with designs for buildings made from 'plug-in' parts, houses that homeowners could carry around and expand, and cities like travelling festivals, made from fold-up buildings that could be packed up and relocated. Back then, this kind of architecture was unbuildable. Fifty years on, though, Cook's ideas seemed eminently

▲ Concrete terraces for the seating are placed on top of the black steelwork.

sensible. His was just the kind of thinking the Olympic Stadium needed.

Sheard calls the Stadium they came up with 'a container for the most spectacular sport and entertainment event in the world'. 'The aim is not to be monumental,' he says, 'not to apply the architectural rules or judge the Stadium by the same values you would judge a coliseum.' Indeed, the Stadium has a compact, intimate interior; its footprint is much smaller than, say, Wembley Stadium. Sheard compares the Stadium to a massive Airfix model. The only permanent thing originally designed

▲ You can see the structure of the whole stadium here – the permanent concrete base and, on top, the temporary elements: the black steel stand, the concrete terraces and the white exterior steel beams holding up the 'ring beam' and lighting rig around the top.

to outlive the Games is the concrete bowl, surrounded by water on three sides and accessed by bridges. The visitor arrives essentially at the top of this bowl, embedded like an upturned hat and raked with terraced seating for 25,000. The entrance, on the podium, is raised well above ground level and covered in temporary stands for food, toilets and merchandise – a strategic location for these facilities which enables the capacity of upper tiers to be reduced after the Games. Dramatic views extend right across the Park.

It is rare for a stadium, especially an Olympic Stadium, to have just one concourse for visitors. This one, though, is very easy to access, through a massive 56 entry points, to reduce queues. The raised podium also allows vehicle access, deliveries and services to

◀ ABOVE LEFT The Meccano-like steel structure of the Olympic Stadium has bolted connections to provide flexibility for future use.

▲ Dramatic shard-like patterns, part of the London 2012 branding, burst across the seating, but still allow the running track to take centre stage.

▲ The concrete tiered seating system is supported by black steelwork, allowing the white superstructure to stand out against a dark backdrop.

be cleverly hidden underneath. Inside the Stadium you can see the threshold between permanent and temporary marked by the concrete rim that circles the middle of the seating. Underneath, in the space beneath the seating on the West Stand, are hospitality rooms, changing rooms and functional spaces for athletes.

Everything you see above this, though – all that seating for 55,000 extra spectators, the white zigzagging steel girders and the lighting rig on top like a sparkling crown – was originally designed to be taken down once the Games are over, and possibly reused. There were even plans right at the start, inspired by Peter Cook's thinking, to use the structure in future Games, with the idea that these might be less about permanent structures and more like a moveable festival made from an adaptable infrastructure, to reduce resource use.

The upper stands, though temporary, have to work hard too. To reduce costs and environmental impact, Populous was compelled to make the structure as lightweight and economical as possible. The black-coloured steelwork, strengthened by the external white zigzagging beams, was put together like Sheard's giant Airfix kit. The terraces of seating, made from prefabricated sections of concrete slabs were dropped on top, and the whole structure tightened up using the circular 800m ringbeam of steel at the rim. This in turn is topped by the roof, a thin membrane of PVC-coated polyester covering two-thirds of the venue and a ring of triangular lighting rigs (each 28m tall) that, from afar, give the Stadium the appearance of a lily flower about to open. 'The idea is to change the rules for the building,' adds Sheard. 'Each piece has its place and its value is judged on its usefulness and the contribution it makes to the whole. The Stadium seeks to be elegant, lightweight, environmentally minimal.'

The Stadium has had to be planned alongside a changing brief. Its long-term purpose was not pinned down before it was designed; thankfully, the design response – a building that can adapt to change – is perfectly apt because, in the end, plans for the Stadium after the Games did change, radically (p.250). Now, instead of being split in two, its 'temporary' stands being demounted to leave its concrete bowl

▶ The Olympic Stadium is oval rather than circular and the seating runs all the way round the running track at the centre, ensuring everyone has great views. You can see the site is almost like an island, bordered by water.

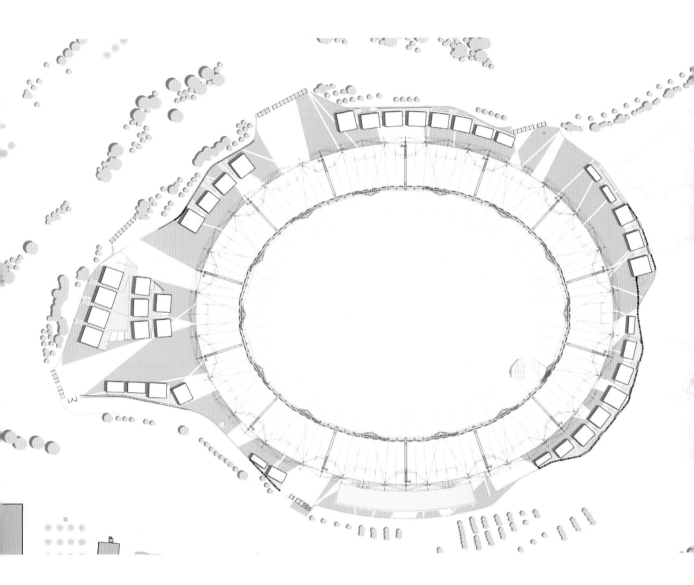

as a permanent athletics venue, the entire Stadium will remain but be remodelled from 80,000 seats to 60,000 capacity. Rather than be sold, it will now remain in public ownership and potential tenants will bid in early 2012 for uses including athletics (it has been confirmed as the venue for the International Association of Athletics Federations World Championships in 2017) and local community sports, as well as a football venue. As so often happens, 'temporary' architecture has ended up becoming permanent. What a good job it has been so expertly and elegantly designed.

▶ Escalators wind up the interior to create a *Bladerunner*-like space, full of soaring vistas.

◀ Two-thirds of the monochromatic seating is covered by an internal canopy and, above it, a lighting rig dances around the Stadium's circumference.

▼ OVERLEAF: The underbelly of the finished structure, shown here in October 2011, can be clearly seen here, showing the Meccano-like building system created from a kit of parts.

Velodrome

The Velodrome crouches, half-embedded in the landscape, like a creature about to pounce. This building is taut. Just look at its haunches, east and west, sticking up in the air like a cyclist's muscly limbs. If any of the London 2012 buildings could be said to embody in form the innate qualities of the sport it contains, it is this one. Cycling is about speed, economy, tautness and an awful lot of whizzing round and round. The Velodrome is called 'The Pringle' by some, the curve of its roof resembling the shape of the potato crisp. Fair enough. But perhaps it seems more like a spinning wheel, one whizzing round so fast that its frame has warped.

No wonder. British gold medallist Chris Hoy was an adviser, and former Australian cycling champion Ron Webb (p.79) designed the track. Chris Hoy played an important role, giving advice and precise recommendations for making a fast track including optimum track temperatures and a completely still air speed. He brought a very practical perspective to the design, for example insisting that a toilet should be positioned as close to the track as possible on the in-field for pre-race preparations. 'The point was to try to communicate the

GAMES CAPACITY
6,000

SPORTS
Track Cycling, Paralympic Track Cycling

DESIGN INNOVATION
The roof is incredibly light – just 1,000 tonnes – around half that of any other covered velodrome.

EXTRAORDINARY FACT
The track, or 'piste', is made from 56km of strips cut from Siberian pine trees, certified by the Forest Stewardship Council and secured with more than 360,000 nails.

PLANNED FUTURE USE
With a reconfigured BMX track, and a new mountain-bike track and road-cycling circuit, will form centrepiece of new VeloPark, a permanent cycling facility for use by the local community and elite athletes, owned and run by Lee Valley Regional Park Authority.

▶ The Velodrome's soaring roof is one of the Park's great design successes. It embodies the poise and drama of the sport.

excitement of cycling,' says its architect Michael Taylor, Senior Partner at Hopkins Architects and a cyclist himself. 'Use the building as a great big amplifier to communicate what's happening on the cycling track to the audience and beyond. We started with the cycling track. The shape of that is a given. But then, the trick is getting the audience as close to the action as possible. So that the building seems shrink-wrapped onto the track.' The two tiers of seats are huddled around the 250m

▲ The Velodrome is built from a concrete base, embedded with a lower tier of seating and topped by an upper stand of seating with a ring beam around the lip. The roof weighs just 1,000 tonnes, so light because of its innovative engineering technique – like stringing a tennis racket. Double rows of steel cables crisscross the expanse in a 'tartan grid' tied to the rim.

track. The lower tier is embedded into the landscape; the upper tier is raised along the flanks by the start and finish lines, where there is more demand for seating. Between the two tiers there is a 3m-high band of clear glazing, so you can see from inside out, and outside in.

The building expresses itself and its contents in a very different way to Zaha Hadid's Aquatics Centre. The latter is all about exuberance, reflecting the brief from the 2005 pre-bid competition which initially included the Water Polo Arena. The Velodrome, briefed later into the Park development, responded to a greater emphasis on sustainability and cost restraints. Expressive in its economy, its designers come from

◀ ABOVE LEFT: Only when the building is made watertight is the carefully crafted racing track or 'piste' built – itself a thing of beauty, developed with former Australian cycling champion Ron Webb.

▲ The Velodrome's cross section is light and simple. This model shows the concrete elements (in white), the wooden façade topped with a steel ring beam and the light, steel cable-net and wooden panel roof that hangs from it.

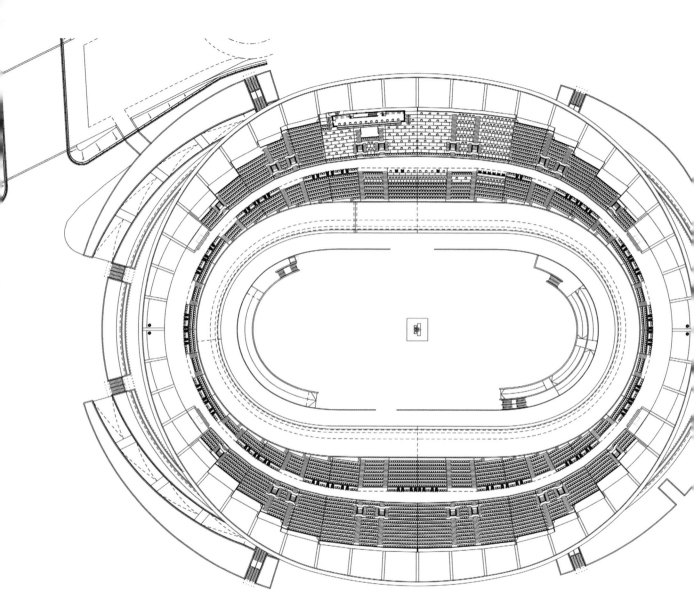

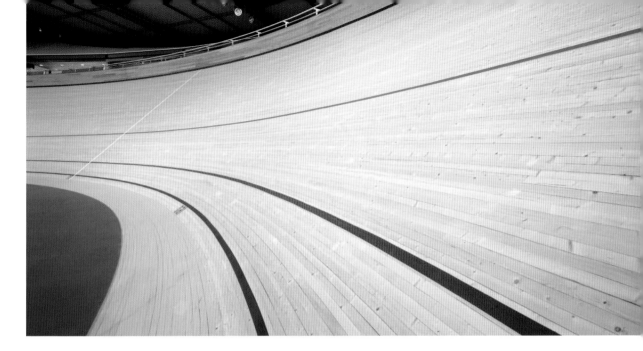

a very different architectural basis. Sir Michael and Lady Patty Hopkins – a generation older than Hadid – set up their firm in 1976. They are 'hi-tech' architects – like their more famous contemporaries Lord Foster and Lord Rogers (Michael was previously in partnership with Foster), designers of London landmarks such 30 St Mary Axe (The Gherkin) and its neighbour the Lloyds building – less concerned with making creative shapes than with solving functional problems technologically and economically. Hopkins Architects, though, have developed their own distinctive language. Hi-tech architecture can be rather chilly and mechanical, with all that steel and glass and muted grey, but Hopkins

▲ The track is a deft piece of engineering created by the best man in the business, former cyclist Ron Webb, who came out of retirement to design it. Its pitch is incredible when seen close up.

◀ OPPOSITE: In this bowl plan, it is clear that the seating is much deeper around the flanks of the track, where the start and finish lines are, and where most people want to sit.

▲ The landscape was designed to reflect the sinuous lines of the Velodrome,
allowing it to nestle snuggly in its environment.

add to this mix more natural materials, such as stone and brick and, here, the red cedar wood of the exterior walls.

Yet this is still a very efficient machine. Look at the cross section: how simple it is, how poised and balanced. Hopkins' motivation is to solve a problem while saving materials and money, and in doing so to create a simple, elegant form.

The architects had originally planned to have a wooden roof, but, to economise even further, a more radical approach was taken with Andrew Weir from Expedition Engineering: to build a roof like a tennis racket. Pairs of steel cables, 36mm thick, 120mm apart, were strung across the expanse from east to west and north to south, in a 'tartan grid'. The cables were tied tightly to the double-curved ringbeam around the building's perimeter rim, which, in turn, sits on slender concrete pillars above the track and seating. Into each rectangle of the strings of the 'tennis racket', a light, heavily insulated wooden panel (or rooflight) was dropped. Then the whole roof was topped off by a waterproof membrane and timber rain screen.

Its economy with materials – and measures such as rainwater harvesting on the roof and louvres in the building's wooden skin (to ventilate without air conditioning) – make it one of the most environmentally friendly of the venues. This architecture is about form and function most tightly intertwined – just like an athlete.

THE TRACK DESIGNER
Ron Webb

Responsible for the Velodrome's cycling track, Ron Webb is an experienced designer who has built more than 60 tracks around the world. Originally a cyclist, fed up of riding on tracks designed by people who had no knowledge of cycling, he started designing them back in the 1970s. For this one, he came out of retirement. An Australian, he now lives in London, so 'I thought I'd better do that otherwise I wouldn't sleep properly,' he laughs. So what makes a good track? Webb is slightly guarded – it's like asking your mum to give up the family Christmas cake recipe. 'It's about making the track easy for cyclists to ride,' he says. The track is a tight piece of engineering – the racing line has to measure exactly 250m. The underneath is designed in a 3D computer programme and fits together on site, with the wooden track laid on top. 'It's northern pine grown in northern Russia in the Arctic Circle,' says Webb. 'It grows very slowly, and very straight.' So did he ride the maiden voyage? 'No, I'd feel a bit silly if I fell off,' he laughs. Instead the privilege was given to youngsters from an amateur club. Will he be watching London 2012? 'Oh God, yeah. I'll probably be critical of the cyclists,' he says.

Aquatics Centre

Some people have likened the gentle curve of the Aquatics Centre's roof to the elegant flex of a dolphin's back, others to a stingray or a curled surfboard, a swoosh or even a rockabilly's quiff. Architect Zaha Hadid herself says it 'was inspired by a diving swimmer'. But whatever you think it looks like, there is definitely no missing it. That is more than 3,000 tonnes of roof up there, 160m long by up to 90m wide, supported in just three places.

You don't appoint a world-famous architect such as Hadid if you want a shrinking violet of a building. She does architectural razzmatazz. Winner of the pre-bid competition, her Aquatics Centre was conceived before economic and sustainability factors became key considerations, yet the venue still balances spectacular design with the maximum possible sustainable benefits. The graceful roof spans three swimming pools – a 50m pool, a second 50m training pool and a 25m diving pool – in a columnless space, enabling the entire audience to see the action unimpeded. Poised at the main entrance to the Olympic Park the building is, as Hadid says, 'meant to be dramatic, meant to be a landmark, a pavilion in a park, and a very exciting building to

GAMES CAPACITY
17,500

SPORTS
Swimming, Diving, Synchronised Swimming, Modern Pentathlon (swimming element), Paralympic Swimming

DESIGN INNOVATION
The roof is supported on tracks and can slide on one end, like a piece of moveable furniture, so that it can shift and flex, side to side, with the weather.

EXTRAORDINARY FACT
The underside of the roof is laid with 37,000 strips of red louro, a sustainable Brazilian hardwood, laid parallel to the pool so that swimmers doing backstroke can use it for navigation.

PLANNED FUTURE USE
Capacity will be shrunk to 2,500 for future use as a major swimming facility.

▶ The undulating roof and column-free space create a dramatic stage to host the Aquatics events. The yellow seating is in the temporary wings and after the Games will be removed, taking the seating from 17,500 to 2,500, with the glazing continued around.

swim in.' Significantly, the design of the Aquatics Centre has helped to coax Australian sports star Ian Thorpe back to competitive swimming. It is perhaps the one building in the Park that almost everyone would consider iconic – something that sears onto your memory in a single definable image.

Two things that you also can't miss during the Games, though, are the massive temporary seating stands 'plugged' into either side of the building. Like the Olympic Stadium, the Aquatics Centre was built for a reduction in capacity after the Games. There was simply no need for a swimming venue for 17,500 spectators after London 2012 was over; it needed to be shrunk by an enormous sevenfold in capacity (far greater than the Stadium) to assume its future role as a local swimming pool. By splitting the Aquatics Centre's Games role from its role in legacy, Zaha Hadid has created a monumental permanent venue transformed at Games-time by two lightweight temporary additions.

The permanent building itself is relatively simple in concept. The pools (all three in a line), their permanent seating for 2,500, back-office rooms, technical equipment and so on are built into an oval ground-level concrete podium that at one end slopes into the landscape and at the other spills out onto a raised plaza. On top of this perches the huge roof structure like a shell, touching the podium only at a concrete wall to the south and two concrete legs to the north. You can see this clearly

▶ The Aquatics Centre's diving platforms are the first entirely bespoke structures ever to be built for an Olympic Games. It took much persuasion; the defiantly elegant result is worth it.

inside the main pools, where the curvaceous concrete of the podium – culminating in the beautiful coffered ceiling in the warm-up pool and the incredible diving board structure, also designed by Zaha Hadid like a series of overlapping tongues and cast in situ – is left exposed. Moveable floors and booms were built into the pool structure before the Games, although they will only be used in the building's legacy role. The underside of the roof, meanwhile, is shaped as a continuous silvery, fish-like skin, lined with strips of red louro timber inside and out, stained grey to pre-empt weathering. From the outside, though, the

▲ The Aquatics Centre pool hall in Games mode. The temporary seating will be removed after the Games, allowing the interior to fill with natural light.

▶ OPPOSITE, TOP: The Aquatics Centre's plan is a simple oval, with the main diving pool and competition pool aligned in one space and, to the left, the training pool.

▶ OPPOSITE, BOTTOM: A slice through the building shows how the bulging roof structure is strengthened with beams like an aircraft wing.

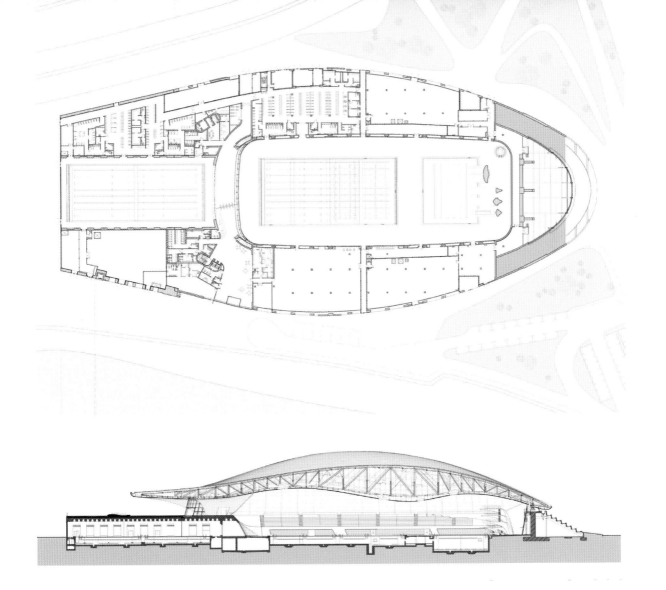

entire form is wrapped in one shimmering, aluminium skin.

It is one thing to come up with such a curvaceous shape on a computer, but quite another thing to build it (p.90). First, numbers have to be crunched, stresses and weights calculated, geometries and the exact arc of those curves worked out. Beneath the roof's skin lies an

▲ The swooping and sweeping shape-making of the glazed window to the pool is the Olympic Park architecture at its best.

▶ OPPOSITE: Concrete is used throughout, and the cast coffered ceilings run not only through the corridors, but also form the ceilings to the training pool.

incredibly complex skeleton – up to 12m deep – engineered by Arup and built by Balfour Beatty, and made from a series of trusses, which fan out from side to side and bulge up and down into a little belly to form the shape. The trusses are made rigid with horizontal and diagonal 'cross braces'. All these elements had to be prefabricated (the steel trusses were fabricated by Rowecord in Newport, Wales, from plate rolled in Gateshead, Motherwell and Scunthorpe), transported to the Park and assembled.

Once the concrete podium was complete, a temporary scaffolding structure was made on top of it and, on top of that, the roof's components put together. Then, once the whole roof was complete, it was raised more than one metre so the temporary support underneath could be removed, before lowering the roof back down onto its permanent columns. That must have been one nail-biting moment.

The building, therefore, has an approach to architecture very particular to Hadid, and very different from both the Olympic Stadium and the Velodrome: the form is as important as function. The sculptural effect of the building is as important as its functional performance as a swimming venue. The form dictates the engineering, not vice versa. It is, perhaps, rather like the arc of a diver. You can see – and be amazed by – its magnificent shape. You just can't witness all the hard work that has gone into creating it.

▶ A dramatic view through the concrete diving platforms to the end of the 50-metre pool.

Park Lives

THE ENGINEER
Mike King

King was the man charged with working with Zaha Hadid's team to make the incredible roof of the Aquatics Centre buildable. This was no mean feat – as project director at engineers Arup, it took him three years from beginning to end. The roof, 160m long and 90m across at its widest point, rests only on two supports at the front, one at its rear – not much to carry the entire weight of this vast, undulating structure. The aim was to make it look 'precariously supported,' says King – 'in appearance' only – while 'sitting very gently on the ground'. Not a job you'd want to get wrong. King's role was to give contractors the confidence actually to build it, so he created a simple engineering solution without diluting its design. 'The challenge was creating a form that looks complex but is made up of a kit of parts,' he says. The whole roof is built from simple trusses and straight elements. 'It's a little bit smoke and mirrors.' Who did King turn to? Bridge builders. In fact, slice the roof down the middle and you'd see a structure just like a bridge. What's he most looking forward to at London 2012? Diving, of course. 'I'm going to shed a tear when they dive off those stunning diving platforms and do a somersault under my roof,' he laughs. 'It'll be the highlight of my career.'

▲ While the roof may look simple and elegant now finished, hidden beneath the cladding is an incredibly complex piece of engineering.

◀ The roof shape echoes that of a giant manta ray, swimming along the seabed.

The Best of the Rest

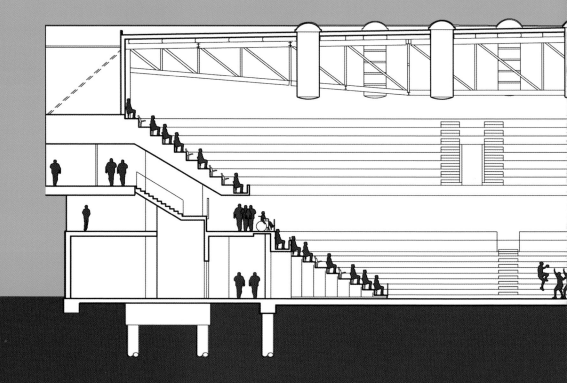

The Park's other venues have so far enjoyed less of the media spotlight. They are less flamboyant and some have a very short life, here only for the Games, but that doesn't stop them being ambitious. Whether they are about making a statement on a budget, transforming their role after the Games or an innovative approach to sustainability, these buildings certainly pack a punch.

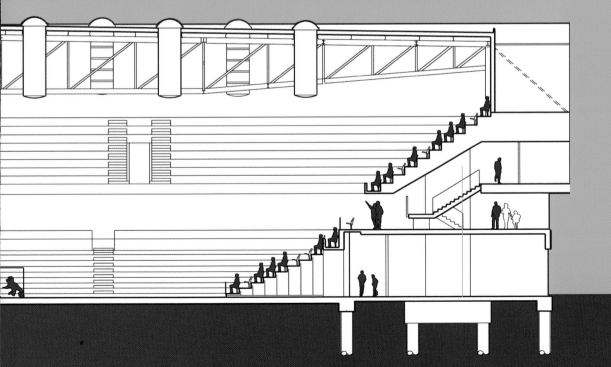

Copper Box

The Copper Box's primary function as a Handball Arena means little to the average Brit. Even its Project Architect at Make, Stuart Fraser, had to do his homework. Around the world, though, Handball is big news. For those unfamiliar with the game, imagine a cross between basketball and indoor football – it's high energy, edge-of-your seat entertainment. And in the Paralympic Games the Copper Box will host Goalball, an equally high energy sport for two teams of three visually impaired athletes, where the ball can reach speeds of 60mph. Played using a ball with bells inside, within a silent arena (so that the players can hear the ball), Goalball is among the most exciting Paralympic team sports.

The design of the arena, in the north-west of the Park, is notably restrained for Make, a practice famed for its flamboyance. Founder Ken Shuttleworth's own house in Wiltshire takes the striking form of a crescent, and since leaving Foster and Partners (after working on the famous 'Gherkin' skyscraper in London's financial district) and setting up his own practice, the studio has become known for big statement buildings, such as Birmingham's Cube. They divide opinion. Yet while the practice began by thinking that their response had to be 'something

GAMES CAPACITY:
6,500

SPORTS:
Handball, Modern Pentathlon (fencing element) and Goalball

DESIGN INNOVATION
Each of the 88 sun pipes in the roof measures 1.5m in diameter and uses an automatic vent to open and close in response to light levels.

EXTRAORDINARY FACT
Eight steel trusses span the roof, each measuring an incredible 4m by 65m.

PLANNED FUTURE USE
Sports competition and entertainment venue for the local community and elite athletes.

▶ The architect has added delight to what is essentially a simple black box with the arena's seating, designed with students from London's Royal College of Art.

wild', says Fraser, befitting such a high-profile commission, they soon concluded that 'there was nothing wrong with rectilinear forms'.

So Make's response was a simple box. 'We started drawing complicated shapes,' says Fraser, 'but it had to be simple, super-efficient, flexible.' The exterior is understated, elegantly clad in strips of pre-oxidised copper, which will develop a natural patina over time. Piercing this metal skin at its base is a strip of glazing running around the entire building that allows glimpses through to the arena – 'almost like a shop window,' he adds.

But Make hasn't become entirely sober and serious. The Copper Box may be restrained from the outside, but inside is where the fireworks happen. Take the concrete interior walls and ceilings, painted vivid red and inspired by 'traditional wooden jewellery boxes,' says Fraser, 'with a red velvet lining', something that slowly reveals its internal treasures.

From these womb-like, red corridors you emerge into a vast, column-less space, with great views from the seats, even right at the back of the first-floor balcony. Brightly coloured, the seats ping out against the dark backdrop. Make worked with students at London's Royal College of Art, finally plumping with them for a random pattern. 'It's a bit of fun,' says Fraser, 'and breaks up the monotony. Even when the venue isn't full, it still has a sense of drama and doesn't feel like a big empty hall.'

The real challenge for Make, though, was to build a venue not just for Handball, but for a range of other sports too, each with their own demands. During the Games it has to shrink from Handball's 6,500 spectators to 4,500 for the fencing element of the Modern Pentathlon, then back up to 6,500 for Goalball – quickly, too. This is crucial even after the Games, when the Copper Box becomes a major community leisure centre, its huge central space used for anything from badminton

▲ Made from a simple steel frame, inside construction of the concrete tiered balcony is seen here underway during 2010.

◄ ABOVE LEFT: Clad in thin strips of copper, the exterior is muted compared with previous work by its architects. Glimpses of red, though, hint at the fireworks inside.

to concerts, as well as elite sport competitions. So, at ground level, the seats are niftily retractable at the flick of a switch; they swing out on a huge arm for certain sports, but can be pushed flush against all four walls for those that require more floor space.

Above, the pared-back, industrial aesthetic continues. Eighty-eight sun pipes are set into the roof to limit the need for harsh artificial light, letting in a third more natural daylight than common in arenas of this size, which 'makes for a much better environment for athletes and spectators,' says Fraser. On the roof, alongside the rainwater harvesting system, these domed rooflights make it feel a 'bit like being stood on the moon', he adds. This may be, as Fraser calls it, 'a robust, tough building', but it still has a dash of the weird and wonderful.

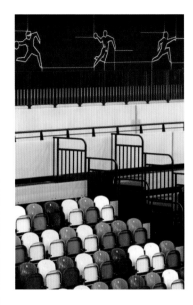

▲ This interior view shows the retractable seating that increases the flexibility of the Copper Box for a wide range of events.

▶ OPPOSITE: All the corridors and circulation areas are painted bright red, again a cost-effective way of brightening the concrete structure and making it more playful.

◀ The ground floor plan shows how the Handball court sits at the building's centre with seating hugging each of its four sides. Visitors enter via the large entrance piazza at first-floor level.

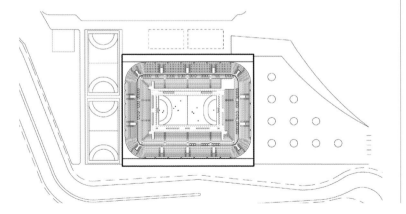

Basketball Arena

The Basketball Arena may be temporary, but it is not a shy and retiring space. In fact, 115m long by 90m wide, 35m tall, dressed in blazing white and looking like a giant inflatable mattress, this arena is rather hard to miss anywhere in the Park. No wonder. The Basketball Arena is one of the largest temporary enclosed structures ever built.

The challenge was to create something simple, cost-effective but more ambitious than a plain white box. Architects Wilkinson Eyre came up with four potential designs, from a Buckminster Fuller-style geodesic dome to a 'plain vanilla' cube, says Associate Architect Sam Wright. But in such a prime, visible site in the north of the Park, next to the Velodrome, 'plain vanilla' just wouldn't cut it. They needed something, says Wright, 'visually stimulating'.

Wilkinson Eyre's final design is constructed from a simple scaffold and is the largest temporary arena of its type ever built. One problem was to find 'the most efficient way of cladding the building', says Wright, with enough bang for its buck. The resulting dymanic façade, a notable achievement, hints at the activity inside as athletes duck and dive on court. Incredibly, this skin is made up of just three modular

GAMES CAPACITY
12,000

SPORTS
Basketball, Handball (finals), Wheelchair Basketball and Wheelchair Rugby

EXTRAORDINARY FACT
Doorways in the athletes' facilities at the Basketball Arena are 2.4m high to cater for the greater average height of the athletes.

DESIGN INNOVATION
Its random façade pattern is created from rotating just three 6m by 25m bays.

PLANNED FUTURE USE
Temporary building; to be dismantled and reused elsewhere, with the site to be developed as the Chobham Manor neighbourhood by the OPLC.

▶ The Basketball Arena's interior is in sharp contrast to its exterior. White and shiny on the outside, inside the dramatic black and orange 'energy burst' colour scheme places the focus on the court.

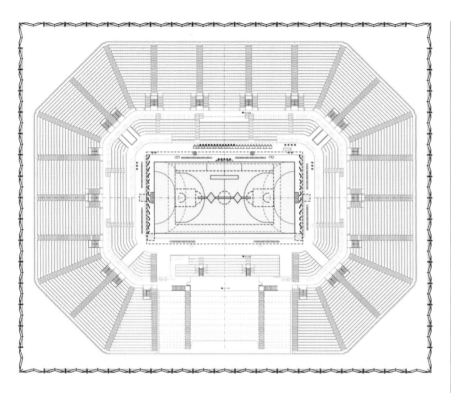

panel designs, each rotated to create an exterior pattern that seems random and bespoke, yet without huge expense.

During the day, when the sun shines, the building will be 'shiny and reflective', hopes Wright. But the real magic happens after night falls. United Visual Artists, which usually works with big stadium acts such as U2, has developed a dramatic lighting show, the building glowing myriad colours, 'kind of like lava', says Wright, to reveal 'an illuminated endoskeleton' underneath.

◀ ABOVE LEFT: The Basketball court sits at the centre of the building, with the raised seating wrapped round all four sides to ensure great views of the action.

▲ White recyclable PVC is stretched over the frame to provide a relief façade, a clever and cost-effective way of adding drama to a temporary arena.

There's no traditional front door, explains Wright. To get such vast numbers in and out quickly and safely, the building is open at ground-floor level, allowing visitors to flood in at various points around its perimeter before ascending to the scaffolded seating bowl running round all four sides.

Inside the Basketball Arena is 'low-tech', using simple materials such as plywood, polycarbonate and recycled plasterboard. Yet the effect is dramatic, from tensile-roof canopies in the corridor linking back-of-house to the arena (harking back to Frei Otto's stadium roof at the Munich 1972 Games, p.23), to the bold black and bright orange seating marked by an 'energy burst' – reflecting an element of the London 2012 brand – that is 'watermarked' across almost all of the Park's seating.

Like temporary buildings across the Park, all the materials are to be reused, from the steel frame to the seats. In fact, the whole building could be reused. 'I'd love to see it at another big event,' says Jerome Frost, the ODA's Head of Design.

▲ Temporary can still be beautiful. The principles of hi-tech architecture have been used to create a simple skin that wraps a scaffold structure. To be consistent with the principle of keeping costs as low as possible, cheap materials such as polycarbonate have been used to dramatic effect.

◀ Coloured lighting will bring life to the exterior of the building and reveal the modular endoskeleton beneath.

Water Polo Arena

With a temporary venue come restrictions, the big one being the budget. When a structure is designed for the Games only, it must be particularly cost-effective. And yet a building that flanks the main entrance to the Park from Stratford City, through which nearly two-thirds of all visitors will arrive – and that sits opposite big structures such as the Aquatics Centre and the Olympic Stadium – calls for some drama.

The Water Polo Arena is no poor relation. Its designer, David Morley Architects, has a great pedigree in creating sports venues throughout the UK – permanent and temporary. David Morley actually found the limitations of designing a building with such a brief life 'one of the most exciting things', he says. 'Could we make something out of the design constraints?'

The architects approached the building 'from the inside out', he explains. Measuring 23m by 37m, the pool is surrounded by 'slightly raised catwalks', as Morley calls them, for the referees to run up and down, following the game. Their height made it difficult to create good views of the action from the raked seating if placed conventionally, on either side of the pool, so Morley devised an asymmetric arrangement

GAMES CAPACITY
5,000

SPORTS
Water Polo

DESIGN INNOVATION
Inflated recyclable phthalate-free PVC cushions are used for the roof instead of a single layer, which prevents heat gain and loss and, therefore, condensation. Each inflated cushion measures 54m by 10m.

EXTRAORDINARY FACT
The venue will reduce water use by 40 per cent, through low-flow taps and showers, as well as waterless urinals.

PLANNED FUTURE USE
Temporary building; to be dismantled with elements reused or recycled, with the site to be developed by the OPLC for residential use.

▶ The building is clad in a shimmering silver PVC wrap which is fully recyclable.

that puts the public on one side and the referees on the other.

The design works well outside too. 'The Arena is conceptually part of a family,' explains Morley, 'alongside the Olympic Stadium and the Aquatics Centre. But with the "wings" on the side of the Aquatics Centre, it's also one of three big temporary structures, so has a powerful resemblance to these.' This relationship forms a 'natural' entrance to the building, says Morley. Entering the Olympic Park over the main bridge towards the Stadium, visitors double back across the River Lea, with the building's entrance acting as a funnel to feed people into the Arena and deliver a splendid view down over the pool.

The exterior is wrapped top-to-toe in a silver-coloured, recyclable, PVC membrane, then topped with large, inflated, self-supporting cushions to form a sloping roof that, thinks Morley, 'ripples like a series of waves'. Phthalate-free, this relatively new product can either be fully recycled or re-used as it is, neatly rolled up without creasing, like a blanket. 'The aim was for 100 per cent recycling,' says Morley. 'We've used standard components, completely demountable, like a Meccano set.' The seats can be removed, and even the piles in the ground unscrewed and reused.

▶ This construction view of the Water Polo Arena shows the dramatic funnel-shaped entrance, reflecting the seating tier within.

▶ BOTTOM LEFT AND RIGHT: These cross-sections show that the roof has a dramatic slope. Inflated cushions help to prevent both heat loss and heat gain.

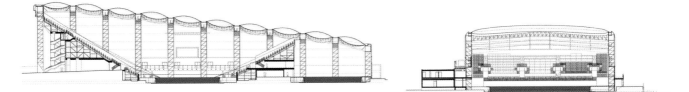

The Riverbank Arena

The open-air Riverbank Arena is the Park's third major temporary structure. When it comes down and the Park reopens in 2013, you'll never know it had existed. Yet like its siblings it has to make an impression during its short life. 'At one corner of the Park is the Olympic Stadium,' says Jeff Keas, Principal at its architects, Populous (who also designed the Stadium). 'At another is the Aquatics Centre. The Velodrome sits at a third, so the Riverbank Arena is the fourth cornerstone.'

Keas's approach is to revel in its position in the far north, with the skyline of both London and the whole Park at its disposal. This is one structure designed for taking photos. Its horseshoe shape was inspired by Populous's earlier PNC Park baseball stadium in Pittsburgh, USA, renowned for incredible views of the city. Here, too, explains Keas, 'we're using the city as a backdrop' – conceptually a fourth façade to the south, where the seating bowl has been lowered especially. This careful positioning connects the city, the venue and the people in one memorable image. When the TV cameras pan round, this will be the 'money shot', says Keas. In a way, it's 'the broadcast material and the photos that will be this arena's real legacy,' he observes.

GAMES CAPACITY
16,000

SPORTS
Hockey, Paralympic 5-a-side Football, Paralympic 7-a-side Football

DESIGN INNOVATION
Expressing and celebrating its temporary nature, with lighting under the scaffold to make the void glow.

EXTRAORDINARY FACT
For the first time ever at an Olympic Games, the colour of the Hockey pitch will be blue rather than traditional green.

PLANNED FUTURE USE
Temporary building; to be dismantled with the pitches relocated to the new permanent Eton Manor sports facility in the north of the Olympic Park and the site used for temporary parkland before being developed by the OPLC.

▶ The Riverbank Arena is a temporary venue designed to be dismantled after the Games. A non-standard blue pitch (usually pitches are green) makes for an arena with a difference.

Like the Water Polo Arena, the Riverbank Arena is constructed from a kit of parts, with a finite number of possible arrangements. 'The language will be temporary,' says Keas, 'but it's about assembling it in an interesting way. We're not trying to hide the temporariness. Temporary can be good, it can delight.' The seating sits atop a scaffolded structure that wraps around a bright-blue Hockey pitch, accessed by several

▼ The Riverbank Arena architect was inspired by their previous horseshoe design for the PNC Park baseball stadium in Pittsburgh from 2001.

entrances into the amphitheatre. While most temporary arenas would be fully wrapped to hide the scaffold, Populous exposed it, to celebrate further its true nature. 'It's an honest approach,' Keas suggests. Like the Olympic Stadium, it's easy from the look of it to see how the whole building fits together.

▼ Great Britain's women's Hockey team train at the Riverbank Arena as the pitch is unveiled in October 2011.

Facilities for the Future

Legacy has proved the stick and the carrot of the Games: sometimes appearing to limit possibilities, at other times to inspire novel flexible solutions. The IBC/MPC Complex, composed of the International Broadcast Centre and the Main Press Centre, and Eton Manor are both venues whose destiny has been hammered out as much by their post-2012 use as their Games function.

Eton Manor

To the north of the Olympic Park is Eton Manor. When compared to the Park's more high-profile international sporting venues, it is decidedly modest in scale and in its architectural treatment. Eton Manor has an important role to play, however, both anchoring the Park in the community and providing continuity for a local sporting heritage. A sports club was first established here in the early 1900s when four philanthropic Old Etonians founded the Eton Manor Boys' Club to give lads from the East End the opportunity to enjoy sport and social activities – everything from boxing, shooting and cricket to amateur dramatics and debating. An important amenity for locals for nearly a century, surrounded by busy roads and the River Lea to the west, Eton Manor had in the last couple of decades become increasingly isolated by traffic. Eventually it fell into disrepair, closing in 2001. For the architects Stanton Williams, who have been involved in redesigning the public realm at Tower Hill around the Tower of London, King's Cross and Sloane Square, Eton Manor was an urban scheme rather than about swanky new buildings. It gave them an important opportunity to provide what designers often refer to as an

GAMES CAPACITY
10,500

SPORTS
Training pools for participants in Aquatics events; Wheelchair Tennis during the Paralympic Games.

DESIGN INNOVATION
Regrading and landscaping of site.

EXTRAORDINARY FACT
40,000 tonnes of reclaimed soil from the Olympic Park were used to re-landscape the site.

PLANNED FUTURE USE
Sporting facilities offering tennis, hockey and five-a-side football for local and regional communities.

▶ One of the Wheelchair Tennis courts built for the Paralympic Games viewed at ground level. Eton Manor's main timber building is to the right, and the Velodrome is to the left.

'urban sticking plaster'. Stanton Williams' priority was to reconnect this island site to neighbouring streets and to the Olympic Park itself, using pedestrian bridges. Fill from the Park was opportunistically repurposed to transform the entire site, raising it 2.5m and screening it from the busy A12 to the south. At the same time the main hockey pitch was sunk into the ground as a bowl, giving the landscape a contoured effect.

Close by the Park but outside its boundaries, Eton Manor has effectively supplied back of house support to the Games. When initially cleared, the site became the temporary home to the Construction College East London, which was a training ground for those seeking employment on the Olympic Park. During the Games, Eton Manor is to be an Aquatics training venue, housing three temporary swimming pools as well as temporary pools for Synchronised Swimming and Water Polo. Only during the Paralympic Games will it become a spectator venue, hosting the Wheelchair Tennis competitions with a capacity for 10,500. After the Games, it will offer a variety of community sporting facilities, including five-a-side football pitches and mountain bike trails.

Eton Manor is also intended to become a centre of excellence for both tennis and hockey, featuring six outdoor and four indoor tennis courts and two international standard hockey pitches relocated from the Riverbank Arena. The main one will have permanent seating for 3,000 spectators and possess the capacity to expand to 15,000

▲ Boys in tweed jackets from the East End enjoying rifle practice at the Eton Manor Boys' Club in the 1950s. The club stood on the site of the current Eton Manor venue.

for future tournaments. A new garden has been designed around a restored war memorial to the Eton Manor Club members killed in the First and Second World Wars. An area for allotments has also been reallocated to replace those previously removed from the site. Fauna and flora are more widely being encouraged with a brown roof of crushed rubble and soil on the main Sports Centre, enabling local wildflowers to seed on it, and through the installation of bird boxes.

For Eton Manor's main Sports Centre, tennis hall and hockey stadium, the architects have employed what they describe as a 'robust architectural language'. This is in keeping with the semi-rural setting and is highly practical, permitting a secure building to be created in a relatively isolated place. It also allows for a great deal of internal flexibility: the organisation of the inside of the building has to respond fully to each phase of its use, whether by wheelchair athletes or local teams. Board-marked concrete has been used for the lower part of the central building and for the hockey seating, while the public upper part of the main building is finished in dark-coloured, smooth aluminium cladding and the tennis hall is clad in Western Red Cedar.

With so many overlapping uses, before, during and after the Games, Eton Manor could be regarded as one of the most complex schemes. Yet its combination of built-in adaptability with an appealing sturdiness should stand it in good stead in the future.

▲ Visualisation of Eton Manor during the Games: the concourse bridge spanning the A12 and Ruckholt Road connects the venue to the Park.

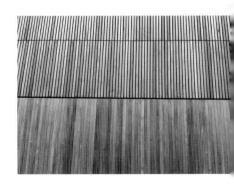

▲ The Western Red Cedar cladding on the main sports centre complex. The timber exterior adds warmth to the rectilinear form.

IBC/MPC (International Broadcast Centre/Main Press Centre)

As the people responsible for communicating the Games to the world, the media have a significant role to play at London 2012. The sheer number of them, though, presents the organisers with one of the greatest challenges. No fewer than 20,000 accredited press and broadcasters are to be accommodated on a relatively small site in the northwest corner of the Olympic Park, squeezed between the A12 and the River Lee Navigation Canal. This is the equivalent of shoehorning in the population of a small town. In fact, in addition to the sophisticated technical requirements within the media work spaces at the International Broadcast Centre (IBC) and Main Press Centre (MPC), the complex has all the amenities of a local mall. It has the parking – a Media Transport Mall, with 1,200 car parking spaces and a coach drop off. It has the catering facilities – a dedicated village, where 50,000 meals a day are to be served. It also has the High Street, connecting the IBC and MPC, which provides a whole range of services from a hairdresser and

GAMES CAPACITY
20,000

GAMES USE
Media centre for international broadcasters and press.

DESIGN INNOVATION
Flexible space planning for Games and legacy use.

EXTRAORDINARY FACT
The IBC is almost double the size of the Tate Modern.

PLANNED FUTURE USE
Business space

The IBC/MPC Complex viewed from the air. The Media Transport Mall and the A12 are in the foreground. Behind it to the left is the expansive mass of the International Broadcast Centre and to the right is the Main Press Centre alongside the Lee Navigation Canal.

The stainless steel piping work of the International Broadcast Centre makes a sophisticated reference to British hi-tech.

grooming centre, massage salon and gym to a dry cleaners and post office. There are also two late night bars, from which reporters and technical staff can order snacks at their desk until 4am.

From the start, the acknowledged discrepancy between the thousands of media professionals using the facilities during the Games and the limited demand for commercial space in this part of east London drove all the plans. (The IBC/MPC site is closer to Hackney Wick than Stratford, so at least 15 minutes walk from a Tube and a main shopping centre.) The initial scheme by the architects Allies & Morrison and the developers Carillion/Igloo was devised to trigger development. They envisaged a whole new media neighbourhood, Soho East, being propagated post-2012 along the canal with a healthy mixture of housing, work spaces, small shops, cafes and restaurants. Hackney Wick was to become another Shoreditch for east London. With the slowdown of the property market and a necessary tightening of belts at the ODA, it became apparent that such a vision was just not in the pipeline. Rather than designing the IBC structure with the focus largely on future use, the building is now being designed for the Games and future-proofed. For instance, when planning the internal spaces of the IBC, the BBC was consulted to ensure that it is suitable to adapt into television studios.

Long enough to house five jumbo jets from wing-tip to wing-tip, the IBC is a great aircraft hangar of a building. It is so big that its steel frame has been designed potentially to break down into three separate buildings after the Games. Allies & Morrison, who designed the envelope (RPS were responsible for the main structure) have made a virtue out of the broadcasters' technical requirements. They have located the extensive mechanical plant used for cooling the studios during the Games on the outside. This breaks up what might have been a long and very dull elevation along the north of the Park and effectively signposts the building's use by placing the services on the outside. This reduced the building's footprint and cost. It also contributed to the flexible design of the building's structure, making it easier to divide into separate units if required by the legacy tenants after the Games. In contrast with the IBC, the MPC, also designed by Allies & Morrison, is a more discreet presence on the Park – workaday in its treatment and provision of office space. A four-storey block with a concrete frame and rainscreen cladding on the outside, it has been designed internally to be as flexible as possible. This makes it suitable for division into small units for start-up businesses rather than simply providing large, open plan spaces for established companies. One of its most innovative features is entirely out of sight from ground level: a 'brown roof' of gravel and moss that attracts invertebrates.

Planning for the future always involves an element of unpredictability. Nowhere has this been more testing than at the IBC/MPC where the changing economic climate has had a direct bearing on ambitions for the area. Across the Complex, however, the architects and the ODA have successfully retained an eye on what is in front of them, rigorously thinking through every aspect of the buildings with potential legacy use very much in mind.

▲ A view of the multi-storey car park in the IBC/MPC Complex. The majority of press and broadcasters will arrive at the Olympic Park by bus or possibly by car during the Games, although the car park was primarily planned for legacy, as Hackney Wick public transport hubs are quite distant.

▲ A view of the International Broadcast Centre from across the Park. The exterior is flexible, allowing for panels to be replaced with glazing if necessary.

Fields of Dreams

The Olympic Park's buildings are only one part of its story. Just as important are the spaces in between them, the setting they are in. In fact the striking design and landscape of the Park are central to its success, both in creating memorable set pieces with innovative planting and public art, and, most crucially of all, connecting the Park to the city around it.

People too easily forget how important that nebulous thing, the public realm, is. Too often it's an afterthought. Yet, in the Olympic Park especially, it is these spaces – the Park itself – in which visitors will be spending most time, in between events, moving from venue to venue, chilling out on the lawns, eating a picnic. After the Games have finished, too, it is the landscape that will provide one of the most enduring and crucial legacies, reborn as the Queen Elizabeth Olympic Park. Over a hundred hectares of lawns, paths, squares, trees and planting are designed to stitch the surrounding neighbourhoods – Leyton, Stratford and Hackney – to the Park and to each other, and as a destination in its own right.

▲ The wetlands in the Park help to create a new habitat for wildlife. Invasive species have been removed and new native species including reed, iris, willow and alder will be able to flourish.

A vital role. Aside from Victoria Park, commissioned by Queen Victoria for the working class of the East End, this part of London has precious little designed green space of any quality. Its long history of industry and relative impoverishment means it lacks the leafy squares lavished on the richer west and centre of the capital, and its grand parks, too, such as Hyde Park, Kensington Gardens and Regent's Park. In years to come, this major new Park in a still economically underdeveloped part of the capital will be where local people come to recharge their batteries, hopes George Hargreaves, of US practice Hargreaves Associates. How does he want people to feel when they visit? 'Inspired,' he replies, after a long pause.

Yet this Park comes with quite a radical agenda, suggests John Hopkins, Project Sponsor for Parklands and Public Realm at the ODA, 'to bring together city design, landscape design, garden design and horticulture all in one space. They're usually separated, but I've always seen them as integrated.' The Olympic Park will draw them back together to create a sort of 'woven' park-city hybrid that is 'liveable, walkable, and connected to the surrounding neighbourhoods', he hopes, making the visitor realise just how close Stratford and Hackney – once divided by industry and the River Lea – really are. Both Hargreaves Associates and the London Development Agency (LDA) were appointed: 'George was the director,' says Hopkins, 'and LDA were the cameramen. George's

experience in Sydney [where he designed the landscape of its Olympic and Paralympic Games in 2000], and in designing post-industrial landscapes counted for a lot. As did LDA's delivery on parks in the UK.'

The key decision was Hargreaves' suggestion essentially to split the Park into two, each with distinct characters. The decision was prompted by the sheer scale of the Park, its sinuous shape wrapped around the permanent venues and, when they're built in years to come, the patches of new housing and neighbourhoods. To the north is the pastoral Park, quieter, taking advantage of the area's greater space; while the south – where most of the London 2012 venues are sited – has a more urban

▲ Wildflower meadows have been planted well in advance of the Games. Here they are in bloom in 2011, creating a romantic setting for the Olympic Stadium beyond.

feel, like that of a large, city park, packed with activity. 'If you have events in a park it attracts people in who perhaps wouldn't have come before,' suggests Hargreaves. 'This is the common living room for the area.' To achieve this, the hard landscaping that is put in for the Games will be retained afterwards as a festival site in the south Park for music and local events where tents can be erected easily. 'We brought the two modes – Games and post-Games – close together, so that there wasn't much change,' he says.

A British park, though, cannot call itself a British park without a celebration of that great national obsession: gardening. This is, after all, the country that gave the world floral clocks, municipal borders, the Chelsea Flower Show and the glories of Sissinghurst and Tresco. To continue the tradition, a design team comprising Hargreaves, LDA, the University of Sheffield and Sarah Price Landscapes has created the 2012 Gardens in the south of the Park, a half-mile long garden filled with trees, shrubs and flowers from around the world. 'This is the part where I consciously said let's celebrate the British garden,' he says. 'I'm fascinated by the plants that you have here, by the heritage of nursing plants for months on end. I appreciate how much that has meant to horticulture design.'

The 2012 Gardens are divided into four – Europe, North America, Asia and the Antipodes – acknowledging Britain's long history of trade, travel and Empire, during which we brought plants back and nurtured them obsessively to create the gardens that make Britain famous. 'It's a fantastic concept,' says Hopkins. 'The Games are about bringing sport and culture to east London. The gardens are about bringing plants from all over the world and celebrating climatic zones.'

Yet there is one thing that truly unites both north and south Parks: the River Lea. Hargreaves wanted to take more advantage of the river and 'knock the riverbanks back'. His idea, essentially, was to reassert the geography of the river. Too often in London's history its rivers have been overlooked, turned into sewers in all but name, or covered up and built upon. It's only in recent years that the city is learning to love them again. The Lea is a case in point, the beauty of its natural floodplain and winding channels long obscured by centuries of building, industry and fencing off by private landowners.

'Everything starts with the river,' Hargreaves says, 'and creating access to it.' The river now acts as a backbone to the whole Park, its banksides creating intimate spots, almost a series of 'local parks, where you can bring your family, your boyfriend', he smiles. Earth has been removed to create, in the north, a bowl cut from the landscape that allows a shallow gradient to run from the top of the Park – this acts as a transition to the Lee Valley Regional Park, lying 30 kilometres to the north of the Olympic Park – down to the river. The excavated earth

has been cleaned and used to create landforms that scoop down, up and around, funnelling you in from the main entrance hub between the north and south of the Park towards the Velodrome – one of the major sports buildings that will remain in the north of the Park after the Games. The landscape responds to the curves of its roof, with sinuous

▲ Aerial view of the River Lea in the Park. The widened river has been planted with reed beds and the banks reinforced with wildflower turf.

lines weaving down to the river. Here you can take glances through the trees and see how the rise and fall of the landscape relates to the surrounding buildings.

Down at water level, the river's wetlands are part of a mission to create habitat for wildlife and manage local flood risk. Biodiversity was a key driver. 'We leave behind 102 hectares of parkland,' says Hopkins, '45 of which is habitat.' To meet this target, the team has put in the largest wet woodland to date in the UK, as well as froggeries, kingfisher banks, otteries and restored marshlands. Other species such as grey heron and water vole will also find a haven in the parklands area, and Hopkins notes with pride that there are 'over 700 individual wildlife areas'. Essentially they have put back much of the landscape that would have been there before industrialisation in the eighteenth and nineteenth centuries. There's a striking visual effect, too. Instead of the hard, man-made division between water and land common in most urban landscapes, there is a soft, picturesque blurring, made up of reeds, shrubs and bobbing moorhens.

This is cutting-edge stuff for landscape design. 'It's not the first example of putting large public events next to a biodiverse landscape, but it is the largest,' says Hargreaves. Traditionally these two approaches have been separate. 'To have the contemporary profession take up the idea of wildlife habitat for all is the way to go.' But for the public, just the simple fact of having such a large, lush and lavish park in the east of the city will be the real legacy of the Games. The UK's largest new urban park for over a century, it offers invaluable space to walk, escape and take a long deep breath.

GREEN SHOOTS

George Hargreaves may be world-renowned, but he's not the only one involved in the landscaping. As part of London 2012's arts programming, a team of artists and designers made up of the University of Sheffield's Department of Landscape, The Klassnik Corporation, We Made That and Riitta Ikonen has come together to design a wildflower meadow, a project called Fantasticology.

It is estimated that around 70 per cent of visitors will enter the Park from the eastern entrance, via Stratford, but the lucky lot who take a path less travelled just to the south, off Stratford High Street, will burst upon a bright carpet of colour. More than 10 football pitches' worth of wildflower meadows, rich in nectar to attract bees, will dazzle those attending the Games. Plants such as cornflowers, Californian poppies, marigolds and prairie flowers, due to flower gold just in time for the London 2012 Opening Ceremony, have been carefully selected by experts from the University of Sheffield to provide a glorious display. The planting, Tomas Klassnik explains, will 'recreate the footprint of

▲ The Greenway runs the length of the Northern Outfall Sewer. The architects won the competition to redesign this elevated embankment as part of London 2012, which acts as a main pedestrian route to the Olympic Park.

THE GARDEN DESIGNER
Sarah Price

Designing the planting for the London 2012 Gardens is a dream commission for anyone, but when your design studio has only been running for two years it's not a phone call you expect. 'I didn't think a practice of this size would get a chance,' says Sarah Price, director at Sarah Price Landscapes. In fact Sarah is one of a small team that has transformed the Olympic Park from post-industrial backwater to a rich, biodiverse landscape. Her role has been to create a 'show-stopping planting scheme', and the team's wider approach has been to do something experimental, 'combining meadow-like plants with more traditional arrangements and colliding different aethestics,' she says. It certainly sounds dramatic. Split into four zones, the planting mix ranges from a soft romantic feel with rich purples and pinks through to spiky planting and vast, lily-like plants that measure a whopping 1.2m tall. 'The feel here is quite Seventies,' says Price, 're-introducing plants that fell out of fashion.' These will be teamed with hot pinks that clash with oranges, yellows and purples. They're 'almost going to shock people!' she laughs, before visitors move into a much calmer area where irises dominate and the colour palette is reined in with plenty of black and white. 'People really respond to colour,' notes Price.

buildings that were on the site before the London 2012 development in geometric patterns and vivid planes of colour.' The idea is to 'connect back to the history of the site, and create a talking point,' he says.

This neat idea most 'reveals itself', says Klassnik, from high up, coming into its own during the Games when TV cameras on cranes and in helicopters swoop over the landscape; or after the Games, when the public throngs the viewing platform at the top of the nearby Orbit and Klassnik's 'logic of the pattern' becomes clear.

The collective has also designed a series of entrance features for The Greenway, a 7.5km-long path that runs the length of the Northern Outfall Sewer – part of the city's Victorian sewerage network created by Sir Joseph Bazalgette and now covered by an elevated embankment redesigned by landscape architects Adams & Sutherland. The improved route opened long before the Games and will remain an important walking and cycling route afterwards. Reclaimed materials have been inlaid to the paths, a theme that was picked up on by the group when they designed their 6m tall entrance markers, which they covered in graphic patterns found on manhole covers in the area. This same pattern has been supersized and created in concrete as 'welcome mats' on the ground, says Klassnik. 'We tried not to do a conventional standalone sculpture, but to embed stories into the fabric of the structure.'

▲ Artists collaborated with the architects to design a series of tall entrance markers covered in patterns taken from nearby manhole covers.

Art in the Park

The East End is famous for its artistic community, so it is not just the sportspeople who have competed to get into the London 2012 Games. Britain's cultural elite have also risen to the challenge, reasserting the ancient but often overshadowed cultural agenda of the Games.

Culture was integral to the Olympic Games in ancient Greece. Even in the early years of the modern Games, in the twentieth century, there were art competitions. This element has gradually withered over time, but the UK, with its spirited recent history of contemporary art, was keen to reintroduce it at London 2012. The Cultural Olympiad will add its own layer to the Games, but it is the Park's public art programme, featuring works designed in from the very start of the process, that will leave the lasting legacy. Of course the showstopper catapulted into the headlines is the 114m-tall Orbit, by Turner Prize-winner Anish Kapoor – its sheer size and rollercoaster-like twists and turns means it will steal the show. But from 'art trees' sporting metal rings to poetry installations to Monica Bonvicini's compelling mirrored sculpture 'RUN', art has been cleverly integrated throughout the entire Park from the start.

'In the same way that three things formed the original ethos for

▶ Anish Kapoor's twisting, turning rollercoaster-like design for the Orbit has captured the public's imagination. After the Games, visitors will be able to access the viewing platform at the top and be treated to a stunning view across the entire Olympic Park.

the Games – culture, education and sport – with the Park it was about bringing together art, design and engineering,' says Sarah Weir, Head of Arts and Cultural Strategy at the ODA. 'The thinking was that art was not just added on, but that it was integral.' The days of a statue plonked in a plaza are long gone. These days it is about weaving art into the physical landscape in all sorts of ways – by collaborations with architects, by literally embedding it in the landscape, by creating art that can be inhabited, such as the Orbit, or by forming creative relationships in the actual process of making the landscape. The point being to add another layer of richness to the complex palimpsest of the Park landscape and connect it spiritually to the East End, which, in the past 20 years, has become Britain's foremost area for creativity in the arts. The perimeter of the Park, especially in Hackney Wick and Fish Island, is dense with artists' studios.

The literary heritage of country and region is celebrated by Winning Words, an innovative programme of poems – some temporary, six permanent – displayed across the Park. Specially commissioned works include Lemn Sissay's 'Spark Catchers', inspired by the history of the Bryant and May match factory at the edge of the Park, and John Burnside's 'Bicycling for Ladies', which links themes of cycling and liberation with material from the archives of Sylvia Pankhurst (a noted campaigner for women's suffrage, cyclist and sometime resident of Bow). A new work from Poet Laureate Carol Ann Duffy will be installed near the Eton Manor venue, while the last line of Alfred Lord Tennyson's *Ulysses*, the first poem nominated in 2011, will be engraved as a permanent feature on a wall in the centre of the Olympic and Paralympic Village.

This clever art strategy of deep rooted integration is the brainchild of Weir, who in her previous role as Executive Director at the Arts Council worked very early on to get 'culture at the Olympic table', and was later asked to deliver her vision. Rather than standalone sculptures dotted about the Park, the work is woven into its very fabric, whether as a bridge, an underpass or even the landscaping. This means that the Queen Elizabeth Olympic Park, as the Park will become after the Games, will not be left with a host of redundant artworks that need to be 'decommissioned', as Weir puts it.

It is a radical and fresh approach to commissioning art for the Olympic and Paralympic Games. 'We're trying to deliver something new for London 2012,' says Weir. 'We looked back to Sydney, where everything that brought the Park together in terms of arts and culture was retrofitted post-Games. Their message to us was that it should be done before.' That set the agenda. The art was seen as a way of 'adding something' to the architecture, of 'pulling the Park together', given that each building had its own unique character.

At a simple level, that was as easy as picking out 12 bridges

▲ The View Tube was built in 2008 as a means of connecting locals with the actual construction of the Games – it's one of the few places the public can get up close and view the building process.

(symbolising the year 2012) and painting the undersides in the London 2012 colours – pink, orange, blue and green – a dramatic counterpoint to the grey concrete or green landscaping. Every art project is about engaging the passer-by, and is either a 'celebration or commemoration of London 2012', Weir says. 'Some will be little reminders, such as the colours under the bridges, a memory of the Games.' Others are bigger gestures at 10 locations that will incorporate artistic 'markers' around the edge of the Park.

'We thought about how people interact with the work,' says Weir. Instead of static artworks, such as a sculpture, many are interactive. The Park's bridges are a key example. *Fast, Faster, Fastest*, by Jason Bruges Studio, encourages people to race against the speed of their sporting heroes (represented by a moving strip of light) across one of the Stadium bridges (p.178). It is an artwork that will serve as a reminder of how the Park began life in years to come. Hackney-based artist Martin Richman has created *One Whirl*, a bridge covered in vast, sweeping circles made from two different colours of crushed glass, inspired by the energy of the Games. 'This could have been plain Tarmac,' says Weir, 'but by doing this we thought people might be intrigued, that kids will follow the circles around. It makes people interested in their environment.' Areas that could have just been 'utilitarian and pretty dull', she says, have been brought to life.

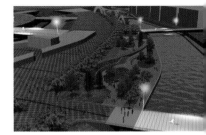

▲ *Fast, Faster, Fastest* is a specially commissioned artwork by lighting designer Jason Bruges. Visitors will be able to race their sporting heroes across a bridge by chasing a flash of light set to the speed of different athletes.

But it is not just the final artworks that characterise the project. Throughout the construction of the Games artists have vigorously worked together with local neighbourhoods as a way of stitching the massive impact of the Games into people's communities. 'People live around the Park, yet can't be a part of it because of the boundary put up during the building work,' says Weir. 'So for them the Games may just mean that their usual bus route has to be diverted, or that there is disruption through dust and noise. They're asking, "Where am I in all this? Where do I fit in?"' A series of artist-led community projects responded to that, such as Memory Marathon, for which artist Simon Pope walked a 26-mile route in one day through the five east London Host Boroughs nearest the Park (Hackney, Greenwich, Newham, Tower Hamlets and Waltham Forest) with a relay of more than 100 local residents, who recalled their stand-out moments from past Games as they went. It was

▲ One Whirl is an artwork conceived by local artist Martin Richman. Huge coloured circles made from recycled glass display the energy of the Games.

◀ From the View Tube, the public can look directly over to the Olympic Stadium from the viewing platform or from the cafe inside.

then turned into a film by Film and Video Umbrella who partnered Pope on the project. This was shown both in local cinemas and further afield while the group continue to stay in touch with each other and the artist.

Floating Cinema saw artists Nina Pope and Karen Guthrie collaborate with UP projects and Hackney-based young architects Studio Weave to turn a boat into a cinema. The artists worked with local people who live on the River Lea, including boat builders, to create films about the area. These were shown on board the boat and at three big outdoor events alongside a talks programme, and included both new and archive footage made by professionals and amateurs. The boat also hosted a drop-in session every week for the local community to see what was going on. 'It's artist-led,' says Weir, 'yet working with people who live and work on the river and outside the Park, and often feel rather swept up or lost in the regeneration themselves.'

The View Tube was commissioned for much the same reason. Constructed from old shipping containers and painted eye-popping lime green, this low-tech structure sits on the Greenway to the south of the Park, overlooking the Olympic Park site. It's been one of the few spots for the public to get up close to the construction in the Park since 2008. 'It's a view, a brew and a loo. A place to see the Park, have a cup of tea and a pee,' laughs Weir, which belies her determination to allow the public access to the changing landscape to invoke a sense of ownership and inclusion.

Alongside specific projects, Weir has also set up an artist in residence programme. Neville Gabie worked from October 2010 to December 2011, with access to the entire site. His 'socially engaged, conceptual art practice', as Weir describes it, focuses on the stories of the people who actually made the Park, such as the man tiling the pools of the Aquatics Centre or the bus drivers who ferry the workers around the Park. His work highlights the 'people that are often very overlooked', Gabie says. 'There are so many jobs and roles crucial to making the Park happen' (p.159).

Involving the community has been at the crux of Weir's vision. 'We've tried to work with local organisations as much as we could,' says Weir. 'My real interest is post-Games. That day when everyone leaves and the Park reopens, we wanted people living locally to feel part of it; to feel that they own it. We haven't added community projects for the sake of it.' Weir will continue the art programme as Director of Arts and Culture at the Olympic Park Legacy Company after the Games, ensuring that 'creative thinking is absolutely part of the Park and that the memory of London 2012 reflects the three Olympic themes of culture, education and sport,' she says.

THE ORBIT

While most projects are integrated, a couple are 'stand out', as Weir calls them. Orbit by Anish Kapoor just can't help it. This project was led by the Mayor of London's office and won through a competition managed by them. It will fulfil the role of 'visitor attraction', says Weir and the desire for 'something that would be some form of centrepiece' in the Park.

It certainly divided opinion when it was announced as the winner, and the blogosphere went crazy with the rants of mouthy detractors. Is Weir worried? 'Only for the first 24 hours when there was silence,' she says, 'and I thought, "Why? What's happened?" That's what art does when it's at its best: the worst thing would have been to have had no reaction.'

OPPOSITE: This in-progress shot shows the Orbit nearing completion in 2011.

Kapoor, who is collaborating with world-renowned engineer Cecil Balmond – famous for making the impossible buildable, such as OMA's looping CCTV headquarters in Beijing and Kapoor's vast Marsyas that filled the Turbine Hall in Tate Modern in 2002. He won, thinks Weir, because his 'artistic concept felt very aspirational, in a very appropriately Olympic way. It's a symbol of modernity and yet has a timeless feel.' She points to how it reflects what is happening elsewhere on the Park. 'It's an extraordinary marriage of art, design and engineering. You shouldn't be able to build this piece, it's never been designed before.'

Technically it's a first, and it reflects London 2012's wider aim to make the Games the most sustainable yet – it is made of 63 per cent recycled steel. At the top of the looping rings of steel will be a viewing platform, which it is anticipated that a whopping one million people per year will visit when it opens to the public after the Games. Accessed by an enclosed lift that allows mere glimpses on the way to the top, the viewing platform is where Kapoor will reveal his signature hand through mirrors – both convex and concave – that will distort and play with viewer's perceptions. From the top you can make your way down through the structure via a winding external stair. 'I think it will be very different when people explore and experience it, rather than just view it,' says Weir. It could well become the next stop on a tour of London's cultural sights.

RUN – LETTERS OF LIGHT

'RUN', by Berlin-based artist Monica Bonvicini, may not have attracted the same kind of attention as the Orbit in the lead up to the Games, but it is a key work, right at the centre of the Olympic Park. Three giant 3D letters spelling out the word 'RUN' sit in a plaza the size of Trafalgar Square, directly in front of the Copper Box. Each letter measures 9m tall, allowing visitors 'to climb over the U and walk under the stalk of the N', says Weir. 'The mirrored glass finish means you can see yourself in

◀ The sculpture, 'RUN', by artist Monica Bonvicini will sit in front of the Copper Box in a giant plaza. Each letter measures nine metres tall and will have a mirrored finish.

it and the surrounding trees.' As the light falls, LEDs embedded around the edge of each letter will glow to create a landmark lightpiece.

While most visitors' first reaction will be that the word 'run' relates to sport, the word is actually taken from lyrics in popular music such as Neil Young's 'Running Dry' and The Velvet Underground's 'Run, Run, Run'. See yourself looking back and 'you'll be slightly startled', says Weir. You'll start to question what the word means to you personally. 'It's not quite what it seems to be,' she says.

The unsung heroes of the Olympic Park are to be found in its infrastructure.

Without these vital parts neither the big, showstopping venues or their more discreetly ambitious cousins could function. The pipes through which water and sewage flow, the cables that transmit the electricity, the bridges to carry visitors across the rivers, roads and railway lines are not designed merely for utilitarian purpose. They've afforded opportunities for engineers to work with architects and artists, in a collaboration that has transformed the humble into the heroic.

Beneath Your Feet, Above Your Heads

The Olympic Park is about more than just the buildings. Beneath your feet, above your heads, this giant beast is supported by a massive investment in a new infrastructure. Of course, you see little of it – it is designed that way. But before even the pipes went in, or the bridges and utility buildings went up, work began on this Games miracle.

For centuries, this vast east London site was a prime industrial area, so the landscape was deeply contaminated with waste. In the old days you would 'dig and dump', as Simon Wright, Director of Infrastructure and Utilities at the ODA, calls it – basically put the contaminated soil into landfill. But these are greener times and, with sustainability a key goal for London 2012, the approach had to be radically different. The entire site was picked over to remove large chunks of concrete and brick, which were preserved and reused or recycled – in fact a massive 98 per cent of all the old buildings on the Park site were recycled by each of the contractors in some way; such reuse and recycling were written into London 2012's sustainability manifesto, *Towards a One Planet 2012*. The remaining soil was then washed – yes, that's right,

▶ The Energy Centre is wrapped in a Corten steel mesh that echoes the industrial railway heritage of the site.

washed – on site, taking an incredible two years to complete, and allowing more than 80 per cent of it to be reused. 'The soil washing was the biggest ever undertaken in the UK,' says Wright.

The other Herculean task was to remove the two runs of giant pylons that once marched through the middle of the site, carrying high-voltage overhead cables. 'It was so urgent that work started on this before the bid was finalised,' observes Wright. 'They were obstructing venue sites,'

◀ OPPOSITE: Abbey Mills Pumping Station by Sir Joseph Bazalgette dates from 1868 part of London's first comprehensive sewerage system. Its high-gothic design is a celebration of the building's importance.

◀ The first major project after acquiring the site was removing the power lines and pylons that marched across it and building two 6km tunnels for the replacement cables.

he says. 'Nothing much else could proceed until they were removed.'

The solution was to bury the cables deep underground in two enormous 6km tunnels that run north to south from West Ham to Hackney, each with a diameter of around 3m – big enough to walk through. This, though, created another problem. High voltage cables can get incredibly hot, so every 2km a ventilation shaft – a headhouse – is needed to let the heat escape. 'Their impact on the Park was little understood at the beginning,' reveals Wright. 'The headhouses are quite prominent buildings,' he notes, and ones in often highly visible parts of the Park. To make a virtue out of necessity, they invited three artists to turn all three into something special (p.174).

Such an attitude is characteristic of the ODA's approach to the Park's infrastructure: don't be embarrassed about it, don't hide it. Make something of it – celebrate it even. In the nineteenth century Britain lavished money and architecture on the humblest of buildings, such as the Abbey Mills Pumping Station, half a mile south of the Park, designed in the fruitiest Victorian high gothic as part of Sir Joseph Bazalgette's sewerage system for the capital. In recent years, though, Britain has become notoriously bad at creating infrastructure – invariably complex and expensive, and usually buried underground or far from public view, with little visible return on your investment. Yet get it right and beautiful infrastructure can add a frisson of delight to a landscape, all the more intense when it is tucked down an overlooked street, just where you least expect it.

All the Park's utility buildings are brave, daring designs. While the big architectural statements – those that house the sporting activities – steal the limelight, these smaller, muscular structures have real integrity. 'They're integral,' says the ODA's Principal Design Advisor, Kay Hughes. 'It was essential they belonged to the site and connected to the area, rather than looking like a shopping centre. It's a high-profile, high-density site. We had an absolute belief these buildings should have dignity.'

Buildings that power the entire site and pump sewage from A to B are hardly fly-by-night structures – they won't simply pop up easily, then disappear like the Basketball Arena and the Water Polo Arena. They're here to stay. There is monumentality inherent to this type of building. Just think of that noble British infrastructural heritage, from Victorian pumphouses peppered across the country to twentieth-century icons such as London's Battersea Power Station. These buildings last. They also prove that the functional can be beautiful.

Once the Games have upped and left, the task turns to transforming the Park into a normal part of the city, a place for people to live in. 'So, of course, we've designed everything for legacy,' says Hughes. 'If we don't create well-designed buildings, we limit the value of the site after the Games.' You can't have an ugly brute spoiling the view for decades to come. 'We were all too aware that our building would [eventually] be part of an urban environment,' says Kevin Lloyd, Project Director at John McAslan and Partners, who designed the largest of the utility buildings, the Energy Centre. 'That there would be housing and offices nearby, that people would be moving past it.'

This range of utility buildings also allowed the ODA to work with private companies to commission younger, less-tested architects, ones with fresh approaches to design. Glasgow-based NORD, for instance, won the competition to design the Primary Substation that sits alongside the Energy Centre. Its powerful, thoughtful design – the first in the Park to win an award from the Royal Institute of British Architects – is one of the landscape's unexpected architectural treats.

As part of London 2012's sustainability agenda, all the buildings in the Olympic Park are ultra efficient. 'Lean, mean and green' has been at the heart of the Games, says Wright. Lean, because building an onsite energy centre has allowed a massive 90 per cent of the fuel used to be converted to useable energy, rather than the usual paltry 40– 45 per cent; mean, because in addition there was a desire to create energy-efficient buildings with at least 15 per cent less consumption than current buildings standards; and green, which was a commitment to produce renewable energy on site. 'We set out a number of key

▶ Battersea Power Station, designed by Sir Giles Gilbert Scott in 1933, was declared a heritage site in 1980. Numerous plans for its redevelopment have failed, but it continues to be an icon, providing a shooting location for numerous films, TV shows and music videos.

targets as part of the energy strategy,' says Wright. 'Fifty per cent of our total energy in the Park must be saved against current standards. That's never been done in Britain. No one has got anywhere close on a project on this scale.'

Such eco-ambition was almost entirely realised with just one building, the CCHP (Combined Cooling and Heating Plant) in the Energy Centre. This green form of energy production that uses waste heat from electricity generation to produce heating and hot water and to drive what are essentially big fridges for air-conditioning. It is a clever piece of kit that in turn affected the design of the Energy Centre (see below), but is rarely used in the UK because of the high upfront costs and slow return. 'No one is ever going to use it unless they are offered an upfront subsidy,' says Wright. 'The Games meant there was a degree of interest. We got round it by joining forces with Westfield [developers of the neighbouring Stratford City shopping centre] who will have high energy demand from day one, and because we're building the Olympic and Paralympic Village we could get private investment to build the energy network with no public investment.' That, in short, demonstrates the power of the Olympic Movement: it encourages Host Cities to think big and to think long term.

THE TRACTOR DRIVER
Andy Atkins

Andy Atkins is just back from a day spraying the Olympic site with water. Now why would you be doing that? 'It's too dry,' he says, deadpan. Ah, of course. The parched spring of 2011 has turned the freshly laid landscape of the Olympic Park into the Sahara, so to prevent Leyton from being caked in dust Atkins has to literally dampen it down. 'I do a little raindance every night.' Just another day in the life of a tractor driver, one of those jobs in which you can be called upon to do anything. Atkins has helped sink shafts for drainage; he's shifted girders; he's carried the shutter moulds used to pour the concrete into for the Aquatics Centre. 'Some of the moulds were £30,000 each; not straight, all carved and everything. My supervisor said, "Whatever you do don't scratch them". The result is fabulous. I used to come in every morning with my fingers crossed — "phew it's still standing!"' Atkins, 63, a resident of Waltham Forest, one of the six east London Host Boroughs, came out of retirement specifically to work for London 2012. He hasn't looked back. 'I saw an advert "How do you fancy working on the Olympic Park?" I thought, "that'd be interesting", better than putting your feet up in front of the telly. I've worked on the Jubilee Line, the Channel Tunnel. Only do big jobs. If it had been anything else but the Olympics I wouldn't have been interested.'

Energy Centre

It may be small, it may not be glamorous, and you won't see it hogging the limelight behind the athletes during the Games, but the Energy Centre is, perhaps, the most important building in the Park. Why? This restrained yet elegant structure – one of a pair in the area, the other east of Westfield Stratford City shopping centre – provides a quarter of the electricity, all of the hot water and heating (as well as some cooling) to the whole Olympic Park, an incredible achievement given its somewhat diminutive size.

Compared to the capital's monumental hymns to power generation – such as Sir Giles Gilbert Scott's world-famous Battersea and Bankside power stations – the Energy Centre is modest. 'We began researching London's history of infrastructure and power generation,' says Kevin Lloyd, Project Director at John McAslan and Partners, 'and became interested in these muscular power stations, built on a large scale to house the equipment of a specific era. The form of these buildings came directly from this equipment, this method of coal-fired power generation. They're durable and hard, but at the same time dramatic and exciting.' That was the inspiration.

USE
The Centre provides energy to the entire Olympic Park and beyond.

DESIGN INNOVATION
Using structurally insulated panels (SIPs) made from recycled timber is incredibly sustainable, and this is the first time they have ever been used on this scale.

EXTRAORDINARY FACT
One of the existing mill buildings on the site is being retained and renovated with space for a visitor centre.

▶ The state-of-the-art Energy Centre provides energy to the Olympic Park, including the Olympic and Paralympic Village.

The Energy Centre responds directly to a very twenty-first century way of generating power: a sustainable one. 'It's a very different generation of power station, one that isn't just producing electricity, but heat and hot water too,' says Lloyd, 'and delivering it locally.' But it, like the stations of old, is also a response to the kit inside. State-of-the art technologies – gas-powered CCHP (Combined Cooling Heat and Power) and biomass boilers that burn waste woodchips to provide green energy – determine the building's size and form. But the design concept also responds to the fact that these new technologies are precisely that – new. Constantly changing at a ferocious pace, the structure has to be flexible enough to accommodate the latest advances in energy production.

This means that the main plant is housed in the large spaces on the southern side of the rectangular building – seen through a glazed frontage, a shop window if you like, that reveals the guts of the building. 'We consciously wanted to let people know what was going on inside,' says Lloyd. The plant is constructed from panels of recycled timber which are then bolted to the steel frame. From this a moulded black rubber box was constructed at ground level, into which aluminium ventilation 'louvres' were fitted that can be easily removed to allow additional plant to be installed as needed. 'The building can be reassembled easily, meaning it is flexible,' says Lloyd.

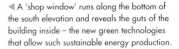
A 'shop window' runs along the bottom of the south elevation and reveals the guts of the building inside – the new green technologies that allow such sustainable energy production.

Running around the 'neutral box', as Lloyd calls it, is a mesh of rust-red weather-resistant (Corten) steel, punched and pushed apart to create a dramatic profile. 'The Corten is a nod to the industrial heritage of the site,' says Lloyd, 'to its rail history in particular.' Flat panels of the material clad the striking flue tower, and help give the building a strong identity similar to the old power stations. Alongside sits an early twentieth-century brick-built factory from the former Kings Yard industrial works, a classic period piece, with beautiful cast-iron columns inside, and the only building from the site's pre-London 2012 past to be retained. It, too, forms part of the Energy Centre, conceived in tandem with the next-door new building to house the Centre's biomass boilers. After the Games, part of it will be transformed into a visitor centre to explain how the Energy Centre works.

Primary Substation

Who would have thought that a simple electrical substation could provide one of the most sublime architectural moments of the whole Games? From the outside, beside the Energy Centre, with which it forms a 'family' of utility buildings, says architect NORD partner Alan Pert, it might look like a 'big, dumb box,' he jokes, but the technology it conceals – and the design – is quite incredible.

NORD is one of the few young architectural firms lucky enough to build something permanent and substantial in the Park, winning an invited competition in partnership with contractors EDF Energy – now UK Power Networks. It relished the opportunity. Most of the Park is built with the architectural attitude of a far older generation: the hi-tech, almost abstract 'scientific' engineering of Hopkins Architects' Velodrome or Populous's Olympic Stadium, philosophically born in the 1960s, say; or the computer-generated form-making of Zaha Hadid's Aquatics Centre, a florid style initially born in the late 1970s. However, in recent years a new approach is slowly revealing itself through architects such as NORD, one consciously reacting to the architecture of their elders by proposing something 'anti-iconic', referencing tradition over novelty,

USE

The Substation distributes electrical power to all the buildings within the Olympic Park, as well as the Westfield Stratford City development.

DESIGN INNOVATION

The architects have cleverly created a building that is just two-thirds the size of a standard substation. It measures only 80m long and 14m wide.

EXTRAORDINARY FACT

The building is constructed from 130,000 bricks.

▶ At night the building glows from inside transforming an industrial building into a thing of beauty.

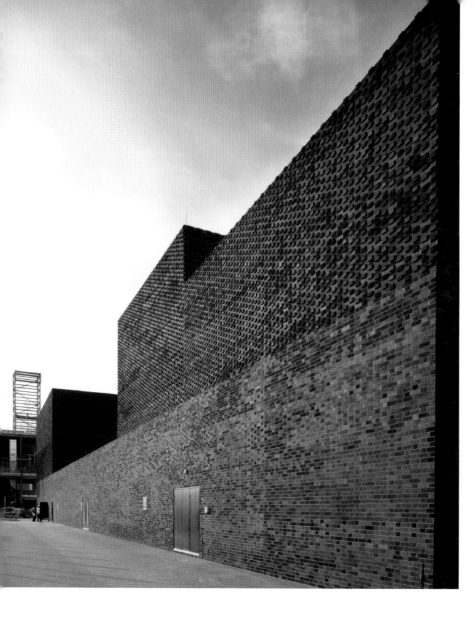

◀ The Electricity Substation is a small but powerful building, its plain brick walls lending it a monumental appearance.

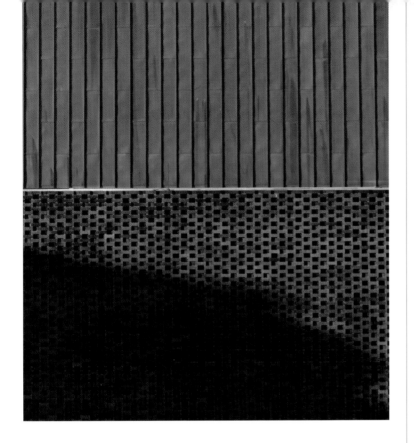

◀ While the materials used are deliberately industrial to reflect the building's use, the black brick has been laid in a delicate filigree. This adds a decorative element to this monolithic structure.

and conveying more about the texture, tactility and history of spaces than about their engineering prowess.

As such NORD's starting point, like that of McAslan and Partners, was London's industrial heritage. 'Much of the debate at the time was about the Olympic Stadium and arenas being adaptable, and potentially temporary,' says Pert. 'But infrastructural buildings like the

Substation will be here for 100 years, they will have a legacy, and so should be built to last.' Through researching Britain's industrial heritage, NORD quickly hit on the idea of using brick. 'Brick is that legacy,' says Pert. As a material that both embodies permanence and references the most famous of Britain's utility buildings, it seemed a natural choice, especially given that the Substation is only 100m across the canal from Hackney Wick, a neighbourhood that proudly displays its industrial brick heritage and in which the Substation will be absorbed after the Games. It's all about context.

The blackness of the bricks, however, came later. Only when NORD had compiled a photo essay of 250 buildings in east London did they realise just how many used black brick, a material commonly used underground and in civil engineering, rather than for civic projects with such a public image. The same black utility bricks were also used around the doors and windows of the original buildings on the Kings Yard site, their inherent strength protecting the openings – one of which remains and forms part of the adjacent Energy Centre. 'While brick was something we wanted to use because of its heritage value, lots of other factors came into play,' says Pert. 'It could be load-bearing, as well as decorative.' Beyond its aesthetic qualities, the Herculean strength of such bricks was a key quality, because the Substation has to be built to cope with certain stresses – for example, if there is an explosion. Recycled London Stock brick was considered, but while it ticked the sustainability box it was not strong enough – so NORD instead plumped for this tough yet dramatic option.

That one simple brick unit can create such different effects is magical. At ground level, and in the cubed buildings at either end, housing the electrical transformers, the bricks are heavy and solid. Yet this traditional brick bond gives way to an elegant lattice pattern above, to create well ventilated spaces for the cooling towers. The monolithic form manages at once to be imposing and powerful, yet, thanks to its perforated skin, also as dainty as your grandmother's doily. At night, the whole building glows from within, allowing you a glimpse of the guts inside.

Continuing that theme common to all buildings in the Park of keeping things as green as possible, a brown roof has been created by covering it in crushed brick, recycled from the previous buildings on the site, which has then been planted with local seedlings to promote biodiversity in the area. The Substation was both the first building in the Park to go through the planning process and the first to complete in early 2010 – though it actually began providing energy to the site in October 2009. It has won three design awards already, including one from the Royal Institute of British Architects (RIBA). Pert wanted to create a 'brave' building. His determination has clearly paid off.

Primary Pumping Station

Pumping stations, in the main, are not considered sexy. Not by most, anyway. Luckily John Lyall is the type of architect who bubbles with excitement at the thought of a building that moves foul water from one place to another. With a track record of designing innovative civil and infrastructure projects such as North Greenwich station, with his previous partner Will Alsop, one of the high-profile projects that was part of London's Jubilee line underground extension in 1997, it is the engineering aspect of a project that gets Lyall's creative juices flowing.

'You have to understand how the engineering works,' says Lyall. 'That's what the design grew from.' The form of the building responds to the circular sewerage chamber beneath, one of a series placed throughout the Olympic Park, linked by a vast network of pipes. It made no sense to design a square building, he says. 'It was a positive strategic move. It meant we weren't digging two lots of foundations, so it also saved money.'

The new pumping station was conceived to work alongside the Northern Outfall Sewer and Abbey Mills Pumping Station, that glorious Victorian Gothic 'cathedral of sewage' just to the south of the Park, part

USE

The building will collect waste water from all the buildings in the Olympic Park, as well as the additional residential neighbourhoods once they are built post-Games. The sewer network is gravity fed and a pumping station is needed to lift waste water up and into the Northern Outfall Sewer for it to continue its journey to Beckton.

DESIGN INNOVATION

It is the first ever circular building of its type in the world.

EXTRAORDINARY FACT

Two large air extraction cylinders housed on the outside of the pumping station have been painted bright pink – site workers have already named them 'Pinky' and 'Perky'.

▶ The first-ever circular pumping station in the world, this sewage plant redefines the modern approach to infrastructure buildings. The bright pink tanks have been nicknamed Pinky and Perky by the construction workers.

of the vast Victorian sewage network begun by Sir Joseph Bazalgette after the infamous Great Stink of the summer 1858, when the appalling state of the capital's slapdash, almost non-existent waste disposal system finally reached the noses of MPs in the Houses of Parliament. The sewer lies beneath the Greenway – a raised pedestrian walkway overlooking the Olympic Park – with Lyall's pumping station beside it at Pudding Mill designed as a chamber to hold foul water, regulating the flow up to the existing sewer.

Abbey Mills is a hard act to follow. No longer are there such vast sums of money to fund public projects. But Lyall's building is cut from similar cloth. An ambitious and celebratory design, it has already won the accolade of 'servicing building of the year' at the New London Architecture awards of 2011. Constructed from concrete – robust, utilitarian, a natural choice, he says, given its ubiquity in the infrastructure business – it is open on one side to reveal two bright pink tanks, 'Pinky and Perky', as construction workers have nicknamed them. These are filled with charcoal through which the fumes from the sewerage beneath are passed and cleaned before being emitted through the 12m tall, odour-control chimney.

'I realised that the tanks would be visible from the train and at ground level, so it seemed appropriate for them to be exposed,' says Lyall. 'I like the idea of the building wearing its heart on its sleeve; by revealing

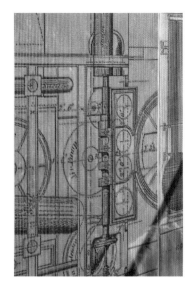

▲ Made from concrete, the surface is etched with engineering drawings of the nearby Abbey Mills Pumping Station (p.152).

some of the "plant" you tell the passer-by what is going on inside.' It was all part of his aim to 'make something utilitarian sexy'. Around the other side, giant 3m high concrete panels – into which images of pumps, valves and pistons taken from Bazalgette's engineering drawings for Abbey Mills have been etched – protect the building. It works. Combined with the glowing blue light that caps the chimney, the building has an attractive robustness, with just enough 'look-at-me'.

▲ At night the station glows, celebrating its vital if under-rated function. The building has been noted for its design excellence, showing a respect for context, innovative and efficient use of resources and setting a new benchmark for utility buildings in London.

The Headhouses

Now here's a problem: where, amid all the thrills of the Olympic Park, are you going to hide three giant 'headhouses' – ventilation shafts to cool the massive underground electricity system, one in the north, and two in the south? They're not exactly shrinking violets, says Alison Nimmo, Director of Design and Regeneration at the ODA, basically 'ugly concrete structures with blast walls, because of all the security issues post 9/11.' No idea? Time for some really creative thinking. Three artists were invited to transform what could have been a blot on the landscape into something that, while still muscular, now at least has added interest. 'What started from not-very-inspiring beginnings has blossomed into something special,' Nimmo says.

In the north, German artist Carsten Nicolai has reinvented what would have been a 'bog-standard metal security fence,' says Sarah Weir, the ODA's Head of Arts and Cultural Strategy, to conceive something ethereal and really rather beautiful. Nicolai, a musician as well as an artist, has created *lfo spectrum* taking inspiration from the five Olympic Rings and imagining them instead as a low-frequency oscillation – the bars you see on a DJ's decks or a synthesiser that

USE

To ventilate the vast underground electricity network, and to provide access for maintenance.

DESIGN INNOVATION

Although more by accident than design (when it was realised just how prominent these structures would be), this is the first time that artists have worked on infrastructure within an Olympic Park making a virtue of what could have simply been ugly lumps of concrete.

EXTRAORDINARY FACT

The tunnels carry 200km of cabling, enough to stretch from London to Nottingham.

▶ Carsten Nicolai's *lfo spectrum* transforms one of the three giant 'headhouses' on the Park.

move up and down according to the rhythmic pulse of the music. This pattern has then been transferred on to the fence in the colours of the sunset at this location – as the sky turns from grey to dark grey then orange. Walk past it and sometimes you can barely see it, while at other moments it catches the sun and reveals itself in full.

At the other end of the Park, Clare Woods and DJ Simpson have used what could be seen as 'the old-fashioned mediums', as Weir, calls them, of painting and drawing to wrap another utility building wall, but in a very contemporary style. Woods has painted abstract landscapes on to tiles, 'honouring the history of the Park', Weir says, as the headhouse sits on the site of an old tile factory. This meets large aluminium panels around the other side, punctured with holes by DJ Simpson to create an image that almost looks like a pencil drawing of the landscape. Where these two very different works meet brings into the sharp focus the 'changing landscape of the Park', says Weir.

◀ This aerial view of Carsten Nicolai's lfo spectrum shows how the artwork conceals what would otherwise be an unsightly lump of concrete.

THE ENVIRONMENTALIST
Sue Riddlestone

'You get a lot of eco-moaners,' says Sue Riddlestone. 'Saying there's nothing sustainable about an Olympic Games, people flying from all round the world to come and so on. My view is, get stuck in. The Olympics is happening whether you moan or not, so make it as sustainable as we can.' Riddlestone is Executive Director of sustainable developers BioRegional, which wrote the environmental strategy for London's bid in 2005. If we have to thank anyone for ensuring sustainability is so high on London 2012's agenda, it's Riddlestone, though she, in turn, modestly praises Ken Livingstone for prioritising the issue right from the start. Together they made sure the One Planet 2012, as it has become known, with its binding five-point plan, was 'mainstreamed' into every single contract, endorsed by WWF and enforced with a sustainability watchdog. Her verdict? 'Sydney was a good effort. Ours will be as good, if not better. Some things we didn't get, like making the Games zero carbon. I'm a bit miffed about that.' But much of the success has been behind the scenes, like recycling demolished buildings and cutting down energy use. 'It's the most holistic strategy ever for a Games, thinking about sustainability not just as an add-on but embedded throughout. The best kind of sustainability is legacy, making sure you invest in the right kind of buildings for the long term. White elephants are such a waste.'

Connections

If there's one thing you can't avoid in the Olympic Park, it's water. For centuries, the Lower Lea Valley's flood plain and many tributaries have proved an obstacle for settlement. In the new Park, though, a problem has become not just a solution, but something to shout about. The water gives the landscape its unique atmosphere, and created the chance for artists, engineers and architects to design a series of beautiful bridges and connections to ensure the river is no longer an obstacle, but an opportunity.

On such a complex site, with waterways and train lines running through or zipping around it, there was never going to be a shortage of bridges in the Olympic Park. 'There are about 30 structures or underpasses,' says Kay Hughes, Principal Design Advisor for Utilities and Infrastructure at the ODA. 'They connect up the elements, stitch the landforms together.' The approach was similar to that of the utility buildings. 'We wanted a family of structures that were relatively simple and blended into the landscape rather than stand out as look-at-me,' says Hughes. The engineers developed a common language of same materials and details to use across the Park. Recycled concrete is housed in metal cages called gabions, and any bridge that passes over a railway line

▶ The stone gabions of the supporting walls of bridges in the Olympic Park are reflected in the polished surface to create an effect not unlike a Hall of Mirrors.

The circular rubber discs create an effect like fallen confetti across the main bridge concourse.

— such as the one that links the site to Westfield Stratford City shopping centre — is made from Corten steel, to ensure it is low maintenance.

A handful of artists have collaborated on six of these, adding depth to what could otherwise be utilitarian structures, transforming the process of getting from A to B into something that you'll rush home and tell your friends about. Local-based artist Martin Richman has designed the central bridge in the north of the Park, covered in swirls of coloured recycled glass, alongside an underpass at the Park's north-east corner, where he has set into concrete small glass beads in bright red and orange swirls that look like giant archery targets.

Jason Bruges, whose illuminated and daily changing artwork wraps around the façade of the new, glitzy W Hotel in London's Leicester Square, has developed an interactive, light-based artwork at another

ABOVE LEFT: Still under construction, the mirrored surface hints at the stunning set piece the bridge will become once complete.

bridge alongside the Stadium, where anyone can race against their sporting heroes. Hit a button, prepare yourself for the countdown and then chase a strip of light that zips across the bridge at the speed of Olympic 100m record-holder Usain Bolt, among others, and see how he leaves you for dust. It is sure to be a hit with the kids. Bruges has also designed two underpasses at the fringe of the site. Light is projected upwards to create an almost pixelated ceiling that, when sensors detect people passing through the tunnel, produce the impression of a swimmer or rower passing overhead.

Beyond the Park's boundary, at Angel Lane, Stratford, close to Westfield Stratford City shopping centre, is a project by London's Royal College of Art students, Oscar Bauer and Nazareno Crea. The Clouds Bridge looks, up close, like a series of pixels; from afar, though, these

◄ ABOVE LEFT: London 2012's art programme provided a great opportunity for rising talent to take part in the Games. Here art students from the Royal College of Art were commissioned to design Clouds Bridge in Stratford.

▲ Interactive lighting designer Jason Bruges has designed a light installation on this bridge to the Olympic Stadium. Visitors will be able to chase light beams across its length set to varying speeds achieved by famous athletes.

small squares inspired by the grid of local high-rise tower blocks focus into a shape, forming cloud patterns along the concrete walls of the bridge, a nod to the great expanses of sky above Stratford and the Olympic Park.

There is, however, one exception to these simple structures. Central Park Bridge is a shiny, shouty bridge with bucket-loads of razzmatazz, designed by Heneghan Peng architects. The competition brief was for two permanent bridges, each about 8m wide, which could be temporarily widened during the Games to accommodate the 200,000 visitors who will pour into this part of the Park each day, past the Aquatics Centre and over Carpenter's Lock to the Olympic Stadium. Dublin-based Heneghan Peng instead created one bridge connected with an elegant 2.6m wide diagonal link – in effect it zigzags across the river in a 'Z' shape, almost morphing up and out of the landscape.

'We felt there shouldn't be a strong separation between the bridge and the landscape,' says Project Architect Andreas Dopfer. 'The bridge becomes part of it.' In what could have been a risky, expensive move, the architects chose to ignore the site boundaries and dig into the surrounding terrain. 'It's at the centre of the Park, and is the hub of all routes. We wanted a bridge that goes over and under, that crosses from north to south, but that also goes up and down,' says Dopfer, linking the upper concourse with the lower

towpath levels. The same concourse surface continues from the Park and across the bridge to create a seamless transition, as though the landscape has simply opened up.

The underside, however, is radically different. Made from mirror-polished stainless steel, the triangular underbelly is like the keel of a

THE CHAPLAIN
Duncan Green

You might not think that religion would play a key role in London 2012. But for Duncan Green, his role as faith advisor has grown from a one-day job to a full-time occupation, heading up chaplaincy services as the Games approaches. The Olympic Park site sits across four diverse, multicultural boroughs whose residents follow many different faiths. 'The two biggest are Christianity and Islam, followed by Buddhism, Hinduism, then Judaism,' says Green. Each is keen to involve its community in the Games, to engage and ultimately to benefit from its legacy. So, what's a typical day? Anything from enquiries about chaplaincy to Muslims' concerns that there will be places to pray and appropriate food during Ramadan, which coincides with the Games in 2012, he says. Green also runs a multi-faith committee where its members discuss 'things that will affect faith at the Games – ticketing, uniforms etc. We influenced putting faith rooms in venues, for example.' However, the bigger goal is to get faiths working together. 'Usually not much gets achieved as different faiths get in the way, but here the common goal has been the Games,' says Green. He'll be one of between 60 and 80 chaplains based on site at the multi-faith centre in the Olympic and Paralympic Village, dealing with anything from homesickness to political asylum to athletes who can't cope with the pressure of competing. 'It's a full-on job,' he says.

ship. Because visitors will walk along the towpath and it will be seen from underneath 'we wanted the bottom to be as good as the top,' says Dopfer. 'In this case, it's even better!' The surrounding sky, river and landscape are reflected in the shiny surface. Cleverly hidden within the bridge are utility pipes that run from the north side of the Park to the south.

During the Games, the 60m stretch between the two end legs of the 'Z' is filled in with a temporary steel and plywood deck to create a vast bridge, approximately 80m wide. This is covered in brightly coloured rubber – the same material that running tracks are made from – in a pattern of intersecting circles in varying sizes. 'We needed to fill it in. What do you do?' says Dopfer. 'We said, "Let's do something that is a bit of fun, that's in-your-face, a celebration." We wouldn't do it for the bridge in legacy mode that will be here in 20 years' time, but it's fun for a few weeks.'

The design's true success, however, is that it is compromised neither during the Games nor afterwards. The confetti-like temporary deck lifts out easily to reveal the permanent bridge and grass-covered bowls beneath – it's as simple as that. 'During the Games, it doesn't seem like something is stuck on, and afterwards it doesn't seem like something is missing,' says Dopfer.

Events from the Olympic and Paralympic Games will take place across the United Kingdom.

The Olympic Park might be where most of the action takes place, but never forget – these Games will encompass the whole country in their excitement and drama. All over the United Kingdom, famous or historic buildings and places, and venues with proud sporting pedigree, have been spruced up and adapted for the rigours of Olympic and Paralympic events.

A National Games

The Lower Lea Valley might be the focus for the Games, but the London 2012 Games is a defiantly national event, liberally spread across the country. Football takes place in Glasgow's Hampden Park, the Millennium Stadium in Cardiff, St James's Park in Newcastle, Manchester's Old Trafford and the City of Coventry Stadium. Sailors brave the waves off the coast at Weymouth and Portland, Dorset, home of the National Sailing Academy; mountain bikers clamber the hills beside the picturesque ruins of the thirteenth-century castle at Hadleigh Farm, Essex; and the rowers flex their muscles at Eton Dorney with Windsor Castle as a backdrop. Even in London, sports are dispersed all over the capital, with Football at Wembley, Gymnastics at North Greenwich Arena, Equestrian at Greenwich Park, Archery at Lord's Cricket Ground, the start and finish of the Marathons and Olympic Road Cycling events on The Mall beside Buckingham Palace, the Triathlon finishing line in Hyde Park, and the Tennis – well, where else but Wimbledon?

A very canny move. By using existing venues you not only save money, but you gain in history, association – and, of course, beauty.

Why build a new venue when Centre Court, Wimbledon is there for the taking? Why not have a spot of Christopher Wren's south front behind the road cyclists in the Time Trial event at Hampton Court? 'The idea of using existing venues as a backdrop emerged early on during the bid for the Games, showcasing both sport and our cultural heritage,' says Kevin Owens, Design Principal at LOCOG. It was this LOCOG vision that formed the brief for Team Populous who then had the job to deliver the project, along with Atkins who provided engineering support. 'It's about using London, indeed the whole country, almost as an instantly recognisable stage set,' explains Jeff Keas, a Principal at architects Populous (designers of the Olympic Stadium) and design and project lead at Team Populous (made up of Populous, Allies and Morrison and Lifschutz Davidson Sandilands), which is responsible for converting these places so they're ready for the practical demands of the Games. Inspired by street parties, its aim was to capture this festival spirit, 'the strawberries and cream factor,' as Keas so nicely puts it. But if there's one occasion when a bit of 'chocolate box' heritage is called for, when Britain can celebrate the history and traditions famous around the world, it is when the eyes of that world are upon it.

Keas and his team are in charge of the temporary transformation of all these venues into Games venues. A gargantuan task. The numbers say it all: a combined capacity of 250,000; 165,000 square metres

▲ PREVIOUS PAGE The Lee Valley White Water Centre sits in a beautiful parkland location. Inspired by the landscape, a C-shaped wooden structure curves round to hold the café and terrace, which looks onto the course.

of tent material; 140km of fencing; and 250km of crowd barriers. Not only that, but they also have to build temporary stands and facilities in some of the country's most beautiful, historic and sensitive sites. And they have to enhance the unique qualities of each particular 'stage set', while ensuring a common London 2012 look across the whole country. Here we highlight the best.

▼ A club runner races down The Mall towards the finishing line at the test event for the London 2012 Olympic Marathon. The iconic backdrop of Buckingham Palace brings a sense of pageantry and spectacle to the occasion.

Greenwich Park,
South-East London

GAMES CAPACITY

22,000, rising to approximately 50,000 throughout the whole park on the cross-country day of the Eventing discipline.

SPORTS

Equestrian events – Jumping, Dressage and Eventing, Paralympic Equestrian; Modern Pentathlon (riding, combined event)

London rarely has those big 'set piece' jaw-dropping architectural moments like Paris or Rome, but this is definitely one of them. 'The finest and most dramatically sited architectural and landscape ensesmble in the British Isles,' UNESCO calls it. There's Greenwich Park itself – a World Heritage Site full of history, where Henry VIII and his two daughters, Mary I and Elizabeth I, were born in a royal palace long since demolished. Yet it is the park's architecture that really stirs the blood. To the south, like a castle on the brow of a hill, the seventeenth-century Royal Observatory – designed, in part, by Christopher Wren. To the north, the Queen's House and Old Royal Naval College Hospital, designed by the greatest architects Britain has ever produced – Inigo Jones, Christopher Wren, John Vanbrugh and Nicholas Hawksmoor. It doesn't get better than this. If anywhere can be said to encapsulate Britain at its greatest, at the birth of its Empire in the seventeenth and eighteenth centuries, a powerful combination of art, science, trade and military might united, it is Greenwich. So quite the backdrop for London 2012's Equestrian events. These buildings have already had starring

▶ The Equestrian and Modern Pentathlon venue will sit on the axis with the Queen's House and has been designed in the shape of a horseshoe to allow magnificent views of the city behind.

▲ Queen's House provides a dramatic backdrop to the London 2012 Equestrian test event at Greenwich Park, July 2011.

roles in endless period dramas and blockbuster films, from *The King's Speech* to *Lara Croft: Tomb Raider*.

The biggest challenge, then, was how to use the backdrop without ruining it. First lesson: don't mess with the programme. Just follow what Jones, Wren, Hawksmoor and Vanbrugh have left for you. 'We have the grand axis, which was understood by Inigo Jones when he placed the Queen's House,' says Jeff Keas of the major route into the park from Blackheath. The temporary, horseshoe-shaped equestrian arena nestles neatly in the dip in front of the Queen's House, and it too emphasises this axis. The city becomes the fourth elevation, says Keas, with the Queen's House, the Old Royal Naval College and the city skyline behind. 'The TV cameras love this,' he adds. Looking the other way, Team Populous kept the seating bowl low enough to be able to see the Royal Observatory from the stand.

The arena is big – 100m long – with a capacity of 22,000. Because it sits within the dip of the hill on a slope, it has to traverse a drop of between 3m and 4m, so an innovative scaffold, developed by Atkins Engineering, set-up has been decked and tested to ensure no vibrations will upset the horses. Most visitors will enter through Greenwich, and will come along the grand axis and through the colonnades at either side of the Queen's House into the grounds.

For the Eventing, the park will host approximately 50,000 spectators – spread around the course. 'The course makes its way around the archaeology,' explains Eddie Taylor, lead venue architect for Greenwich Park, of the Roman remains also on the site. 'It's a minimal touch. The park will return to how it was,' explains Taylor. 'If we do our job right, the legacy … there won't be one. You won't even know the Games were there.'

▲ Inigo Jones' Queen's House in Greenwich Park, with the Royal Naval College behind designed by Christopher Wren with Nicholas Hawksmoor, John Vanbrugh and James 'Athenian' Stuart, is one of London's most famous landmarks.

Lord's Cricket Ground,
North-West London

GAMES CAPACITY
5,000

SPORTS
Archery

Cricket, of course, is not an Olympic sport, but it requires of its grounds two attributes vital to another sport that is: a level playing field and good sight lines. Lord's, the international home of cricket (where its rules and regulations are set), also has a backdrop known around the world from decades of TV broadcasts. The main pavilion – a fruity, red-brick building with wrought-iron balconies and stout, statuesque, square towers by cinema designer Frank Verity – sits beside the 1930s Allen stand, the 1987 Mound stand, by Hopkins Architects (of London 2012 Velodrome fame), Grimshaw Architects' 1996 grandstand and finally, the one you really can't miss, the 1999 giant white aluminium pod of the Media Centre, designed by Future Systems. A rich and very British hotchpotch of old and futuristic, conservative and radical.

Lord's seats more than 30,000 people. But Archery only requires a capacity of 5,000. 'Spectators would be jingling round like change in your pocket!' says Jeff Keas. Team Populous began with a simple question. 'What makes Lord's Lord's?' says Keas. 'The main pavilion.' But because archery must be played on a north/south axis, to prevent

▶ During the Games, two temporary stands will be erected on the cricket pitch to create a more intimate venue for Archery. This creates an axis that links the two architectural set pieces, the pavilion and Media Centre.

◀ Directly opposite the pavilion sits the media centre, a brave commission that garnered much acclaim, so much that it won the Stirling Prize in 1999.

archers from shooting into the sun, at Lord's this meant the field of play would be set on a diagonal across the pitch. To showcase the pavilion and the media centre to the TV cameras more successfully, Team Populous went back to the drawing board and, together with the LOCOG design and sport teams, managed to convince the International Archery Federation to move the axis 39 degrees south, revealing both buildings. At this time of the year, because the sun sets late, this solution wasn't a problem for competitors. The architects then placed temporary stands on the pitch at either side of the pavilion so that 'it feels more intimate, and creates a buzz'.

◀ OPPOSITE: Lord's pavilion is as British as it comes. Victorian red-brick splendor, with delicate wrought-iron terraces – the perfect spot for a cream tea.

Horse Guards Parade,
Central London

GAMES CAPACITY
15,000

SPORTS
Beach Volleyball

It is the centrepiece of British government, with Downing Street for a neighbour. It is where the Queen troops her colours every year during her annual birthday parade, where Britain as a nation remembers the contributions of its soldiers on Remembrance Sunday, where guardsmen on horseback sporting Busbies and peculiar hats perform all manner of traditional ceremonies, and where William and Kate's Royal Wedding guests passed through en route for Westminster Abbey in 2011. For London 2012, however, it will be home to a most un-British sport: Beach Volleyball. Tonnes of sand will be shipped into Horse Guards Parade to create a sight more associated with Bondi Beach than the stiff, sober heart of the British government.

Thousands of people will come to watch Beach Volleyball in the historic centre of London. Some perspective: that's 'like placing Wimbledon's Centre Court in Horse Guards Parade,' says Peter Richardson, lead venue architect. To accommodate such huge numbers, the lower seating bowl of Team Populous's temporary arena runs around four sides, with an upper tier using another of those horseshoe shapes

▲ Horse Guards Parade is where the Queen celebrates her birthday and the Government runs the country. But for the Games, it will play host to Beach Volleyball.

to show off the surrounding architecture and allow views through to a more recent London icon, the London Eye. Again, its temporary nature is part of the aesthetic. 'As we developed the look of the Games, we quickly realised the mantra should be communicate, don't decorate,' says Kevin Owens, so much of the structure is on show rather than wrapped up and out of sight. There is one main court and two warm up courts, with six training courts located in St James's Park opposite. One thing is for sure, it promises to be a surreal sight.

▲ From the stands, visitors will have a great view not only of the action, but also of Whitehall and the London Eye beyond.

Eton Dorney, *Berkshire*

GAMES CAPACITY
30,000

SPORTS
Rowing, Canoe Sprint,
Paralympic Rowing

Not many schools have their own rowing facility. Not many schools, though, are like Eton College – whose sporting achievements include four-times Olympic champion rower Matthew Pinsent as part of their Old Boy network. In effect Eton acts as an unofficial feeder school to Oxford and Cambridge's famous annual Boat Race – its crews peppered with former students. How do they achieve such success? With world-class facilities and teaching that, of course, don't come cheap, funded by Eton College's school fees. Incredibly, though, it is the world's largest boat club, with more members and boats than anywhere else. So its world-class facilities and boat house, newly rebuilt in 2006 by a local Eton practice, HJ Stribling & Partners, are the perfect setting for the Olympic and Paralympic Rowing and Olympic Canoe Sprint, especially with Windsor Castle romantically positioned high above the River Thames as a backdrop.

The rowing lake at Eton Dorney is 2.2km long, the course 2km and eight lanes wide, with a separate return lane. There are two pre-existing permanent buildings – the boathouse and finish-line tower, so, for the Games, little needed to be done. With some 30,000 spectators

expected, much of the work has gone into getting people on and off site. The main entrance has been moved to the opposite end of the venue, and a new temporary Games-time bridge will cross the Thames to allow visitors to enter from the south-east, close to the finish line. However, the main enhancement is a new 50m permanent bridge, designed by architect Ramboll UK (formerly Whitby Bird), that has been created at the finish line area. Further work has included widening the entrance from the rowing course into the return lane to allow boats through much more quickly, and to create a cut through from the return lane at the 1300m stage to make a shorter course for some events, and to line the lake with seating and standing space for spectators. 'The majority of what we're doing is at the finish line,' says Keas. The key is to 'activate the final 250 metres of the course to create the feel you get at a regatta.' A hospitality pavilion will be placed there, designed with balconies and terraces so that spectators can spill out and cheer their support to the rowers as they race to win that all-important medal.

▲ The 2.2km rowing lake is part of Eton Colllege, and has been enhanced to cater for London 2012. Temporary seating and pavilions will line the waterfront during the Games.

◀ ABOVE LEFT: The rowers begin at the top end of the lake, and row towards nearby Windsor Castle, meaning that this historic building is sure to provide a great backdrop to the TV coverage.

Lee Valley White Water Centre, Hertfordshire

GAMES CAPACITY
12,000

SPORTS
Canoe Slalom

The only brand-new London 2012 facility that the public has been able to use before the Games, the White Water Centre was completed in December 2010 and opened to much fanfare in spring 2011. Pictures were plastered across the press of journalists experiencing the course for themselves, sporting hard hats, water rushing and gushing around them, smiles on their faces. While the centre will be used for the action-packed, adrenalin-fuelled Canoe Slalom during London 2012, it is for white water rafting and canoe slalom before and after the Games. Anyone – from elite canoeists to members of the public – will be able to book in and take a trip down the exhilarating rapids.

'There are very few examples of this kind of facility,' says Mike Hall, Partner at its architects, FaulknerBrowns Architects. 'Not many people know what a canoe slalom is, other than it's rushing water.' Given that its roots are in mountain streams, 'to bring it to a flat, urban area is a challenge,' he says. Instead of relying on nature and gravity to shift the water downhill, 'you need pumps and a lot of energy.'

Set in Hertfordshire parkland 30km due north of the main

▲ The only brand-new building designed beyond the Olympic Park for the Games, the Lee Valley White Water Centre is 30km outside London in Hertfordshire.

▶ The snaking courses can be set to many different levels of difficulty, meaning that before and after the Games it will operate as a public facility and cater for everyone, whether Olympian or novice.

Olympic Park, the Olympic course is a 300m stretch of fast-moving water, teamed with a 160m intermediate/training course where the athletes will warm up and down. Rather than feeding off a river, as our current National Watersports Centre at Holme Pierrepoint in Nottingham does, it is a closed-loop system operated by pumps. 'We looked at the ethics,' says Hall. 'We're using water which uses a lot of electricity to move it, so we looked at the most efficient way of doing this.' Making the course sustainable post-Games was key too.

These issues set the agenda for the building and landscape, once they had established the infrastructure and system of loops. The C-shaped timber structure curves up to finish in a terrace that looks out over the course and parklands. MVVA landscape architects were responsible for embedding the course sympathetically in the wider parkland setting surrounding the Centre. They also incorporated ecological elements such as creating new wildlife habitats. 'It's like a piece of landscape that wraps up and over and contains the terrace and café,' notes Hall. Athletes, and the public, will climb into their boats at ground-floor level in an open courtyard, and then travel up a conveyor belt to the first floor, where they have 'wonderful views', Hall says, towards London and Waltham Abbey, before they drop into the start pool and begin.

Thousands of temporary seats will be added to the course for the Games. 'Compared with many other London 2012 venues, quite a

 Terraces, such as this south-facing one, make the most of the centre's setting in a beautiful parkland location.

lot is temporary,' explains Hall. Access to the actual centre will be limited, and the experience 'quite different'. Team Populous worked with the architects to make sure the course functioned from a sporting perspective. 'We put the fans in front,' comments Keas, 'and have tried to get them as close to the action as we can. But we've ensured it's a fantastic experience for the athletes, as well as the spectators.'

As with all the permanent buildings for the Games, it 'was driven by the legacy need,' says Hall. 'The course remains exactly the same,' he notes. 'If this remains as an Olympic sport, it needs to be popular and affordable to provide funds for on-going legacy.' Given that it has been described to Hall as 'the best of its type in the world' by the International Canoe Federation, it is not surprising that he thinks, 'this, along with the Velodrome, will be two of the most popular legacy facilities after the Games.'

ExCeL, *East London*

GAMES CAPACITY
40,000

SPORTS/EVENTS
Boxing, Fencing, Judo, Table Tennis, Taekwondo, Weightlifting, Wrestling, Boccia, Paralympic Table Tennis, Paralympic Judo, Powerlifting, Sitting Volleyball, Wheelchair Fencing

There's a deeply pragmatic spirit to planning the London 2012 Games. Why build something that will only stand empty in the future? Seven Olympic and six Paralympic sports needed a venue that had to be temporary, indoors, with lots and lots of space, handy for the Olympic and Paralympic Village. Conveniently, the ExCeL exhibition centre was a couple of miles south. Now if there is one thing the ExCeL centre has, it is space – vast hangars of space, built beside the water on the quayside of the former Royal Victoria Dock in east London, once the trading heart of the British Empire. Huge though it was, ExCeL didn't have *quite* enough space. It was already planning to double in size, so the expansion was fast-tracked.

Grimshaw Architects' new extension is certainly an improvement on the old, architecturally. A considerable amount of natural light now penetrates the space, a boon in a building type – a conference centre – normally defined by vast but dark and enclosed halls. The new entrance is a jolly, bright yellow, e-shaped spiral, and the stairs up to the first floor help visitors immediately to orientate themselves. And, yes, it is big, containing, indeed, the longest public corridor in

▲ ExCeL's hangar-sized spaces will be transformed into venues for no less than 12 Olympic and Paralympic sports, catering for between 60,000 and 80,000 people. Each hall will be blacked out, with spotlights focusing on the action.

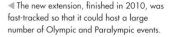

The new extension, finished in 2010, was fast-tracked so that it could host a large number of Olympic and Paralympic events.

Europe, measuring almost half a mile – the Grand Boulevard – and housing retail and leisure space.

But big enough for the estimated 60,000 to 80,000 people who plan to visit during the Games? LOCOG extensively studied crowd modelling to see how this massive boulevard will cope when the throngs – from a number of events being held simultaneously – spill out, or hang out in the cafes from the five hangar-like sports halls it has built alongside it, four of them 10m from floor to ceiling, the fifth a massive 15m. Each holds between 5,000 and 10,000 spectators. Everything is blacked out inside, with spotlights only on the field of play. 'It's like a black box theatre,' explains Ana Paula Loreto, venue architect, 'with the same dramatic atmosphere.' A mixture of seating styles has been installed to allow the best views of each sport – proscenium-style for Table Tennis and Weightlifting; 360-degrees for Boxing and Wrestling; banks of seats on either side of the arena for Fencing and Taekwondo.

The Royal Artillery Barracks,
South-East London

In the eighteenth and nineteenth century, Woolwich was the centre of the arms industry that fuelled Britain's imperial expansion, just downriver from the nation's traditional naval centre at Greenwich. The perfect spot, then, for the Olympic and Paralympic Shooting events. Arms manufacturing has long since disappeared, and Woolwich itself has struggled to find post-industrial purpose and prosperity, but it is blessed with an incredible and little-known architectural heritage from these golden years, such as the Royal Artillery Barracks. The barracks were built between 1776 and 1802 by James Wyatt, the most successful architect of his day who was responsible for designing Kew Palace for George III as well as numerous houses for the aristocracy. A grand building, its long façade is made up of six barracks joined together to form two symmetrical wings either side of a central triumphal archway. It's an eye-popping mix of white stucco teamed with Flemish brick, Tuscan colonnades and myriad coats of arms. It used to sit among three riding schools, stables and a theatre, though only the military accommodation remains. It is still a designated military training area.

▶ The Royal Artillery Barracks were built in the late eighteenth century and were occupied in part by the Royal Artillery until 2007. The Royal Arsenal was also sited here, and for more than 200 years was the Government's principal armament manufacturing facility.

For the Games, three temporary indoor rifle ranges designed by Berlin-based Magma Architecture have been built to the south of the splendidly named Ha-Ha Road – the main entrance for spectators – which bisects the site from east to west, with the three shotgun ranges to the north. The largest rifle range sits closest to the road and holds the 10m and 50m ranges, with the 25m one tucked just behind – both are semi-enclosed. As the finals range is the only one where filming will take place, it is fully enclosed, and since, as a consequence, the designers didn't need to take account of the sun, there was greater freedom about where to place it. 'We wanted to create a hub at the road,' says Keas, responsible for the masterplan of the site, 'which is why we've seated this arena and the shotgun ranges back to back.'

Typically ranges are lined up in a row, with a formal layout. But the designers 'wanted to create a park-like experience,' explains Eddie Taylor. 'A very formal layout fought against the rest of the site, and we wanted to create a sense of enclosure. If we weren't careful, people were going to rattle around,' he says of the site's grand size. The informal feel also derived from technical reasons, to do with fitting the ranges on the site and accommodating the fallout from the shotgun pellets, requiring shotgun ranges 12 degrees off north rather than the due north required by international rules.

Magma Architecture's design of the range buildings is dramatic.

They are large – the site itself is the size of the Olympic and Paralympic Village – and these buildings, says Richard Arnold, Project Sponsor at the ODA, 'are two or three times the size of some of the buildings in the Olympic Park.' Instead of being constructed from scaffolding, like so many other temporary Games buildings, these huge structures are made from a steel frame over which fabric is stretched. They look rather like wedges of Swiss cheese, their skins perforated with giant holes – which allow air through – to reveal bright orange, pink or blue beneath.

▲ The temporary rifle ranges look like blocks of Swiss cheese, each with a different bright colour showing through the holes, which allow air in and out of the building.

Village
People

The land has been cleared, the infrastructure built, the venues completed and the Park laid out.

Only one thing is still missing: the athletes who will drive the Games. Creating the Olympic and Paralympic Village in the middle of a global financial crisis was not the only challenge. Far greater was how to create a place not only comfortable for the athletes during the Games, but which could also transform itself afterwards into a living part of London.

Olympic and Paralympic Village

You would be forgiven for thinking the Olympic and Paralympic Village was built for the Olympic and Paralympic athletes. Not this one. That's not to say the 23,000 athletes and officials won't be housed in impressive accommodation. Nor that the Village isn't perfectly positioned for the athletes' convenience: it is the closest Olympic athletes' village ever built to the actual sporting venues, meaning sportspeople can stroll to work (or sprint, if they prefer), rather than spending crucial minutes before an event cooped up in minibuses. But in this particular Village, the athletes and officials are simply temporary residents, passing through like holidaymakers in a summer resort. It is the more permanent residents for whom this Village has been built. The athletes and officials are just borrowing it.

'It was always designed to create a new community and to give something positive back after the Games,' says Paul Hartmann, Project Sponsor for the Olympic and Paralympic Village at the ODA since 2007. 'It was designed for legacy, and we've incorporated as best we could the requirement of the Games.' Legacy. That's a word that gets

▶ This particular design was taken from the architect's own paintings. Bright and colourful, some have said they look like towels thrown over each balcony.

trumpeted at Games HQ like no other. And rightly so. These Games are all about what is left behind after the Olympic and Paralympic whirlwind has left for its next destination. London 2012 has learnt from previous Games and is determined not to be left with white elephants, resolutely making every pound that the country has forked out count. You *have* to build new accommodation for the athletes and officials – where else are you going to put them? It has to be secure, safe, as well as comfortable. But why waste money building sturdy homes to tear down later, when they could last for decades, or centuries even?

▲ Eleven residential blocks have been built in time for London 2012, and form the Olympic and Paralympic Village. A main east-west boulevard runs through the development and connects with the Olympic Park at the far end.

So the Village, in effect, is east London's latest residential neighbourhood, designed from scratch. It will be joined – in future years, when the legacy company takes over the whole Olympic Park site – with five other new residential neighbourhoods to be built all over the Park by private developers on the sites of the temporary venues, the idea being that the surrounding wider city and the vast Park start to blur into one another. One such neighbourhood is planned just to the north of the Village, on the site of the temporary Basketball Arena, and the Village development itself is planned to expand in a second phase.

This was the last part of the Olympic Park jigsaw to fall into place, and the one major piece designed and built not by the ODA but a private developer, Lend Lease. So just imagine what happened in autumn 2008, just as the Village was being planned, when the world was plunged into economic turmoil. The idea had been for Lend Lease to set up the largest-ever residential fund to build the Village, recouping its investment after the Games when the homes were sold to its new permanent residents. But the economic collapse suddenly threatened the project's business plan. With British property prices slumping and credit well and truly crunched, securing financial backing from the private sector on favourable terms was not possible. Instead, the ODA intervened, securing the development with its own money, with Lend Lease becoming the agent. The final third of housing will now be added in legacy.

▲ A life-size reproduction of the British Museum's ancient Greek Elgin Marbles features on this façade.

Ricky Burdett, Professor of Urban Studies at the London School of Economics, Chief Adviser on Architecture and Urbanism for the London 2012 Games, and now advisor to the Olympic Park Legacy Company, was brought in to lend his expertise, to ensure that within the limits of available time and money, as much architectural ambition could be salvaged as possible. It was a thin and hard line to tread – on the one side, cost; on the other, quality. You want something built on time and within budget, but without sacrificing the quality of a place destined to be absorbed into the fabric of London as soon as the Games were over. Burdett and Hartmann's quick-thinking intervention ensured that design remained at the heart of the project.

Architects were revisited from the long list done for the previous masterplan for the site and following advertisement by Lend Lease. This led to the appointment of 19 practices to design the Village, a mix of larger firms with experience in this kind of development, such as Lifschutz Davidson Sandilands, big names such as Eric Parry and Denton Corker Marshall, and rising British architects, such as Niall McLaughlin, DRMM and DSDHA. 'If there's any richness and grain in the Village, that came out of working like this,' explains Burdett.

With the government, not private finance, now footing the bill, the emphasis was as much on public good as commercial nous. Affordable housing currently makes up 49 per cent of the total, and is now peppered throughout the site rather than shoehorned into the less attractive spots (this figure will reduce to 30 per cent across the entire development when complete). 'That was very important to fight for,' says Burdett. This basic structure means it will better resemble the normal mix of the city that surrounds it and, hopes Burdett, will encourage 'people of very mixed backgrounds and ethnicities' to live there; 'we'll avoid becoming a middle-class ghetto.'

The difficult part has been, of course, to anticipate what this new community, which won't even exist for years, will need. The development has a new health centre, by Penoyre and Prasad, which is to become a community health centre once its Games-time role as

◀ Each residential block is built around a courtyard, which is landscaped to provide outdoor space to residents.

a medical and doping control centre is complete, and a new school, Chobham Academy, by Allford Hall Monaghan Morris (AHMM), which will be used as offices and recreational gym facilities for athletes at Games-time. Shop, café or restaurant units have been built into the ground-level of the blocks. Each block is made up of between six and eight buildings constructed in a square layout set around a large green courtyard roughly the size of four tennis courts. These are mostly made up of one- to four-bedroom apartments, although there are also a number of three-storey town houses too that come with their own gardens. The masterplan dictated that the development had to follow the feel of London's existing streets. The houses with their own front doors were added to the development to create a direct connection with the street.

At 40 hectares, its footprint is considerably smaller than recent Olympic and Paralympic Villages at Beijing (66 ha) and Athens (110 ha). The 11 residential blocks rise up to between 10 and 13 storeys, most of them either side of a wide central boulevard that runs east-west from the Academy at one end of the site to the Olympic Park at the other, which allows great views across the wetlands to the Velodrome. Hartmann claims such high density reflects the 'grain of London', though these blocks are of a bulk more common in the denser parts of central London than Leyton and Stratford. Their bulk reveals that pressure Burdett talks about, between creating a part of the city with the right feel, and piling as many homes as possible on to the site in order to maximise a profit in the future to recoup the public investment.

Indeed, that thin line between cost and quality, delivery and excitement, is at its most visible in the architecture of these blocks. Because they had to be built quickly. So the approach to all 11 blocks is similar: a concrete frame cloaked in a variety of precast concrete and rainscreen cladding, all designed according to pre-determined guidelines of colour palette, density and approach. 'We didn't want a zoo of buildings, but rather buildings that relate to each other and importantly the landscaped spaces between,' says Hartmann. The buildings therefore share a common language, using a natural palette that will wear well over coming decades. While it was encouraging that younger architects were used in the Village, they were partnered with more experienced architects, their contribution often limited to choosing the façade.

Yet even within this very restricted brief, the architects have responded with interest. Eric Parry has thrown in a rare touch of colour by reproducing some of his own brightly coloured paintings on the balconies of his own building – some people love them, others think they look like beach towels thrown over the balustrade to dry.

Lifschutz Davidson Sandilands has had some fun cladding its building in terracotta concrete panels. But it is Niall McLaughlin who has gone the furthest, by turning a problem into a virtue. With Glenn Howells Architects designing the structure of the block, McLaughlin's role was reduced to creating the skin. So he has made the absolute best of it, celebrating the façade-ness, if you like, of his façade, and making it as three-dimensional and architectural as he can with life-size reproductions of the Elgin Marbles. He makes what might have looked flimsy and appliqué seem monumental, timeless and substantial. It will, though, divide opinion, particularly among the older generation of old-school modernists, still suspicious of decoration for decoration's sake.

However the urbanity of the Village – little moves, like the width and proportion of the pavements, the alignment of the roads, balconies on the blocks – is its greatest success. The landscaping should greatly add to this. 'It was key to appoint landscape architects at the same time as the architects,' says Burdett. 'The spaces in between the buildings are the most important.' The Swiss landscape architects appointed, Vogt, have a good track record, balancing well those demands of quality and interest, and practicality and cost. A huge, green open space the size of Trafalgar Square sits at the development's centre, perpendicular to the central boulevard, which will form the heart of the community. At the Village's south-west corner, Vogt has designed wetlands to link

◀ OPPOSITE: This block will be the tallest in the Village, providing 120 apartments for athletes and officials, and then homes for local people after the Games.

◄ An aerial photograph shows the Village at the start of 2012. The main east-west axis runs from Chobham Academy, the round building on the right, to the Olympic Park at the other end, with the Basketball Arena sitting to the top right.

seamlessly with those of the Olympic Park. 'It was crucial to make sure that Vogt's landscape actually connects to Hargreaves' open landscape plan,' says Burdett.

For the Games the Village will, of course, be strictly out of bounds to the public, reserved solely for the athletes and officials who will share its homes and use its civic buildings, such as Chobham Academy, as social centres and canteens. But come 2014, following an 18-month transformation period, the Village will be absorbed into London, to become home to thousands of families. 'We'll take out bits and pieces we put in for the Games,' says Hartmann. Kitchens need to be added, extra bedrooms will be turned back into lounges, partitions taken out to create larger bedrooms.

It is only at this point – or a year or two after residents move in – that the success or failure of the Village will become apparent.

The planners, though, have created considerably more elements for community cohesion than is common in normal British commercially driven housing developments. 'The ingredients are place-making, education, employment, connectivity, entertainment, private gardens and public space – and how you control that – together with health and wellbeing,' says Hartmann. There will be a focus on youth and the elderly too, with community facilities such as a computer club and a rent-a-room scheme for meetings. The ambition is to wean people off private transport: down the road there's Stratford station, with its knot of train lines, as well as Stratford International station; there will be a car pool, in which you can rent rather than buy your own, rented cycle pools and innovations new to the UK, such as full and accurate electronic transport information throughout the Village, so that you know when your bus will actually turn up.

The Village also abuts the new Stratford City shopping centre to the south, built by Australian developer Westfield, which opened in 2011; not a Games project, but, of course, created in concert with London 2012's plans. There's certainly no ignoring it. Its influence will be enormous, essentially creating a vast new town centre for Stratford, glittering with high-end shops – the Village will basically become its neighbouring suburb to the north, with Stratford International station the bond. Phase two of the Village's expansion will expand it significantly around the station – with commercial and residential blocks and towers planned, although their design is far from being finalised.

For Burdett, it was important to ensure 'much more integration between the design of public spaces and the rest of the neighbourhood. I try to think of outside in, rather than the other way round,' he says. To aid this, wherever possible key buildings such as the health centre and school are placed at crucial points linking the new with surrounding neighbourhoods, and within 'an easy walk to the housing areas,' he says. 'Wherever there's an opportunity to make a connection [to the existing neighbourhoods], this masterplan has dealt with that. If you place some of the facilities there it automatically means that the kids from Leyton and Hackney come. Once that happens, it makes all the difference. You have a greater sense of affinity with a place if you walk past it every day.' Burdett believes strongly that you either design a wall around a community, as they did at Canary Wharf, or you encourage transaction between communities. At the Village he has gone for the second approach.

The Village has had its problems, for sure, but its bone structure, its urban DNA, if you like, is good. All that is left now is for its residents to move in, put flesh on the bones and give life to these best-laid plans.

THE LANDSCAPE ARCHITECT
Irene Djao Rakitine

Creating a whole new district from scratch is some challenge. Usually neighbourhoods develop organically over time. But at the Olympic and Paralympic Village, Vogt Landscape was charged with turning 10 hectares of brown mud into stunning landscape in just 18 months. 'It's always difficult to give life to a brand-new district when you build in one go,' says Irene Djao-Rakitine, Head of Vogt's London office. Vogt's concept was to bring a huge axis through the middle of the Village, running from east to west and paved in Yorkstone, traditionally used in London's grand central squares and streets. To avoid that just-finished look, mature plane trees have been planted along the boulevard measuring an impressive 12m high, as tall as a four-storey building. In total, there will be more than 3,000 trees. 'Which is a lot!' laughs Djao-Rakitine. So how will it feel? 'One of our aims is to try and create a warm place,' she says, 'and avoid a sense of a corporate place. The materials are quite warm, and much better quality than normal public realm in England.' Djao-Rakitine is most proud of this. The financial crisis meant massive cuts, but Vogt redesigned everything to ensure quality. Materials won't be thin pieces of cladding but massive chunks of granite. What a refreshing change.

Chobham Academy

Now here's a challenge: design a school, only a school as yet without any headteacher, board of governors or even any pupils. AHMM has a serious track record designing British schools: its Westminster Academy made the 2008 Stirling Prize shortlist. But the Chobham Academy does not plan to open its doors until September 2013, while the neighbourhood immediately surrounding it in the Olympic and Paralympic Village won't fill up with people for some years, at first drawing its intake from Leyton and Stratford down the road.

So how do you design a building when you don't know who will inhabit it? You make it as flexible as possible – the classrooms can be easily moved around as needed. Built to accommodate 1,800 children, Chobham is an 'all-age' academy for pre-school children, infants, juniors, secondary pupils and sixth formers. In effect it is a campus, albeit a small one. The three- to eight-year-olds 'are in a world of their own', says Turner, a low, rectangular, single-storey building to the south-east. In the middle sits the dramatic, central, four-storey drum for the middle and secondary schools. But all age groups share the common spaces, including the canteen, sports hall

GAMES USE
National Olympic and Paralympic Committee and Games organisers' offices, and recreational gym facilities for athletes.

DESIGN INNOVATION
The classrooms are cooled sustainably by taking the rooms' stale, hot air and passing it through a system of 11 'earth tubes' each measuring up to 150m under the playground.

EXTRAORDINARY FACT
The circular form draws civic focus to this community building, in the same way that the elliptical drum of the Royal Albert Hall is a cultural marker on the south side of Hyde Park. Chobham Academy's main building would fit perfectly inside the Royal Albert Hall.

PLANNED FUTURE USE
An all-age academy for the Olympic and Paralympic Village and existing local communities.

▶ An aerial view of Chobham Academy nearly complete with the main circular academy building to the rear, and the lower-school building to the front.

and theatre, housed in a third building to the north-west.

Yet this campus also has to sing out to this community it hardly knows. Schools are the most important civic buildings in any neighbourhood – not just the first architecture we experience as children, but the glue which either binds or divides a place. Especially here. The academy has a potentially tricky 'in-between' site, high on the eastern edge of the Olympic and Paralympic Village, looking across to the Victorian terraces and postwar social housing of Leyton. AHMM, though, has turned this to its advantage, creating a building designed to link the new part of the city with the old. This is a Janus-faced building, looking both ways. 'We're not lavishing all the money on one entrance,' says Turner. Instead, there are many 'front doors'. The bold circular form of the main building both announces itself as a civic building distinct from the right-angled residential blocks of the Olympic and Paralympic Village (it cups a surprisingly intimate square at the end of the Village's main axis), and extends a welcome to Leyton over its sports fields.

On the outside, the building's skin is a rather muted but jolly green. AHMM couldn't afford expensive glass, so a cheaper alternative – full

▲ The four-storey Chobham Academy as it nears completion in 2011.

of iron, giving it its green colour – has been made into a virtue, too, and backpainted with white paint to highlight its minty tone. Three stairwells punctuate the main drum, painted internally in bright red, yellow and orange, glimpses of which can be seen from the street. The building for the youngest children is a simple rectangular pavilion, on the streetside overhanging the pavement while, on the other, exposing its supporting columns on the slope down to Leyton. The third building has a saw-tooth roof with rooflights to bring light into the sports hall. Inside the main circular building, a lofty atrium runs the whole height of the school – each floor is colour-coded, the balustrades taking on one of the colours of the Olympic Rings, with the floor providing the black. A library sits right at the top, with an outdoor terrace offering great views on all sides.

More dramatic than the design, though, is how the school will be used. New schools are required to work hard even after lessons have ended, as 24/7 community buildings. Local residents can use the sports grounds, and even specially designated changing rooms accessed through a separate entrance, a trick AHMM pulled off at Westminster Academy. Its cafe will be open to all at the weekend. Community meetings and adult education classes are planned for when the school is closed to pupils, and the theatre has its own entrance for local events as well as school performances.

▲ Cowls run around the entire façade. They funnel fresh air into the building yet have been integrated into the design to make them into a feature.

Polyclinic

The temptation with any high-profile project is always to think big, sometimes too big. Like so many architects working on the Olympic and Paralympic Games, Penoyre and Prasad's 'initial reaction was to go for something iconic', says Project Architect Mark Rowe. Bright colours sing out on both the outside and inside, a zingy yellow running around – and marking out – the entrance, and punchy lime on the inside, including the floor. But with thought and sensitivity some of the wackier ideas were sensibly reined in. 'I think we've kept some of that,' he says. 'We had the idea of Manhattan where you find a small church nestling among all the tall buildings, and its jewel-like quality makes it stand out.'

'Otherwise, it's a restrained and sober building,' he adds. A monolithic structure clad in white brick, the health centre sits on a triangular plot beside the Chobham Academy, one of the eastern gateways to the Olympic and Paralympic Village from Leyton. The roofline dips down and up asymmetrically along the long entrance façade, welcoming visitors from both directions. 'Even if you're as far away as the Stadium, this distinctive prow will be seen and framed by the buildings on either side,' Rowe hopes. The entrance is through a

GAMES USE
Medical and doping control centre.

DESIGN INNOVATION
The Propane R290 gas chiller units installed to provide cooling have a Global Warming Potential of just 3, as opposed to a hefty 1,400–2,000 for normal chillers.

EXTRAORDINARY FACT
The porcelain powder that makes the bricks white comes from Staffordshire, but is added to German clay in Frankfurt where the bricks are manufactured, making it a truly international effort.

PLANNED FUTURE USE
Primary healthcare and community centre, run by NHS Newham.

▶ A visualisation of the Polyclinic which sits at the edge of the Village site – its users will come from both within the Village and the surrounding neighbourhood. The entrance façade dips down in the middle to welcome visitors whichever way they approach.

recessed arcade that steps back from the line of the building, marked by that bright yellow trim, but which also uses a colour palette of gold, silver and bronze – a reference to the Olympic and Paralympic medals. 'It's a little bit cheesy,' jokes Rowe, but it looks good, the gold and bronze painted glass panels set into window frames, with silver metal fins in between. It's subtle, yet serves to 'lift' the building, which risks being overwhelmed by architect CF Møller's brick apartment block opposite.

'For community and healthcare use, the ground floor is priceless,' says Rowe. This is a building that has to be approachable, right on the street level. Inside, a bright, open-plan reception welcomes visitors with floor-to-ceiling windows covered with gold-painted brise-soleils (shading devices), looking out onto the street one way and onto a courtyard garden the other. 'All your destinations are visible,' says Rowe. Colour is used as a way-finding tool, so the receptionist can direct you, say, to the floor with the big yellow, or green, wall. It beats the confusion of signage common in complex healthcare buildings. The colours run throughout the building, but elsewhere it's used in a restrained manner. On the floor is terrazzo – a posh touch in a building type where budgets are all-too-often squeezed.

'Right from the beginning we said this should be an exemplar,' says Rowe. 'Let's do everything properly.' The compromises have been few. It is a hard-wearing, flexible building that can be adapted to suit whatever uses the Community Development Trust throws at it once it moves in alongside the NHS after the Games. And it was delivered in just two years, at least a year less than is normal for such a building. Which goes to show what can be achieved if the political will is behind a project.

◀ The main entrance leads into a bright atrium. Patients will be directed to the correct floor through the use of bright colours as way-finding tools, instead of simply relying on complex signage.

The Show Must Go On